Also from Quippery

FUR & GRRR
THE FUNNIEST THINGS PEOPLE HAVE SAID ABOUT
DOGS

FUR & PURR

THE FUNNIEST THINGS PEOPLE HAVE SAID ABOUT
CATS

Created by
Craig and Erich Pearson

A **Quippery**™ BOOK

The Funniest Things People Have Said

Quippery LLC
Fairfield, Iowa 52557 USA

ISBN 978-1-949571-02-8

© Copyright 2018 by Quippery LLC

Published in the United States by Quippery LLC

Since this page cannot accommodate all the copyright notices, the copyright notices appear at the end of the book.

Cover design by George Foster, www.fostercovers.com

Printed with chlorine-free ink, on acid-free paper, supplied by a Forest Stewardship Council certified supplier.

www.quippery.com

FUR & PURR

CONTENTS

PROLOGUE
OUR QUEST FOR THE FUNNIEST THINGS PEOPLE HAVE SAID

THE ISLAND

We had spent more than a year sailing along the inner circumference of the Mediterranean, moving counterclockwise. We'd started at Gibraltar and traveled along the northern coast of Africa, then up along the Levant and around Turkey and Greece. Over the last month and a half we'd sailed around the long boot of Italy.

We'd stopped at every port village and city, pulled into every harbor, speaking with the local people. Some stops yielded what we were looking for, but not often and not much. As always, it was like panning for gold.

Now we were heading southwest, along the southern coast of France — Nice, Cannes, Saint-Tropez, Marseilles — lovely, historic cities.

Our maps showed a tiny island, little more than a rock, it seemed, several hundred miles from the coast.

We looked at each other and each knew the other's thought: No stone left unturned.

The island was maybe half a mile across. The only inhabitants we could see were gulls. A lonely and unpromising place.

Tying the boat to a rock, we began climbing upward to get a better view of the island. We made our way among the boulders, myrtle and olive trees swaying in the breeze. Grasshoppers chirped by the thousands. Shimmering blue extended around us to the horizon. Light and heat pressed down from above.

Close to the top, a colony of squawking white gulls suddenly flew straight across our path, ten feet in front of us. They appeared to emerge from sheer rock.

Looking closer, we saw that, in fact, they had flown out from a hole between a group of boulders.

We were able to move some of the boulders aside — discovering, to our amazement, an entrance leading downward into a cave. We descended through the narrow passageway. Thirty feet in, the cave opened into a wider expanse, its granite walls sparkling.

And what we saw there, illumined by shafts of light from overhead, left us stunned.

Arrayed before us were chests filled with golden coins . . . hundreds of bars of unpolished gold . . . buckets of diamonds, pearls, and rubies . . . golden tiaras, necklaces of precious stones, jewel-encrusted goblets.

"Are you thinking what I'm thinking?" one of us said.

"The hidden treasure of the Count of Monte Cristo."

"Which everyone believed was fictional."

"Perhaps — but apparently the treasure wasn't."

"The book says that Edmond Dantès found this after he escaped from the notorious Château d'If."

"Where he'd been imprisoned for life after being framed — on the eve of his wedding, no less."

"And that's where he met and befriended the Abbé Faria, who educated and trained him — "

"And who told him the location of a fabulous treasure — "

"Which made him rich — using only a fraction of it, evidently."

"And which he then used to get revenge — brilliantly."

We stood regarding the treasure in silence.

Again we sensed each other's thought.

"This is not what we're looking for."

"No."

"We're looking for the funniest things people have said."

"And none of this is that."

So saying, we walked up and out of the cave, rolled the boulders back in place, descended through the rocks to our boat, and climbed in.

* * *

Look for more adventure tales in each Quippery book.

IN THE BEGINNING

Scientists say the first cats lived in Europe and Asia about 25 million years ago — just last week, evolution-wise — and that all felines, including lions and tigers, evolved from this animal.

Known as a Proailurus, it was a lot like our modern house cats — same size, same long tail, same large eyes, same sharp teeth and claws, same habit of scratching the furniture. It also spent a fair amount of time in trees, which meant lots of calls to the fire station.

But there are other theories about how cats originated.

On the origin of dogs and cats

And Adam said, "Lord, when we were in the garden, you walked with us every day. Now we do not see you anymore. We are lonesome here, and it is difficult for us to remember how much you love us."

And God said, "Child, I will create a companion for you that will be with you and who will be a reflection of my love for you, so that you will love me even when you cannot see me. Regardless of how selfish or childish or unlovable you may be, this new companion will accept you as you are and will love you as I do, in spite of yourselves."

And God created a new animal to be a companion for them. And it was a good animal. And God was pleased. And the new animal was pleased to be with Adam and Eve and wagged its tail.

And Adam said, "But Lord, I have already named all the animals in the Kingdom and I cannot think of a name for this new animal."

And God said, "As I have created this new animal to be a reflection of my love for you, his name will be a reflection of my own name, and you will call him DOG."

And Dog lived with Adam and Eve and was a companion to them and loved them. And they were comforted. And God was pleased.

And Dog was content and wagged its tail in appreciation of its beloved masters.

It came to pass that an angel went to the Lord and said, "Lord, Adam and Eve have become filled with pride. They strut and preen like peacocks and they believe they are worthy of adoration. Dog has indeed taught them that they are loved, but perhaps too well."

And God said, "Verily, I will create for them a companion who will be with them and who will see them as they are. The companion will remind them of their limitations, so they will know that they are not worthy of adoration."

And God created CAT to be a companion to Adam and Eve. And Cat would not obey them. And when they gazed into Cat's eyes, they were reminded that they were not supreme beings.

And Adam and Eve learned humility.

And they were greatly improved. And God was pleased and Dog was happy.

And Cat didn't give a damn one way or the other.

— Unknown

On the first day . . .

On the first day of creation, God created the cat.

On the second day, God created man to serve the cat.

On the third, God created all the animals of the earth to serve as potential food for the cat.

On the fourth day, God created honest toil so that man could labor for the good of the cat.

On the fifth day, God created the sparkle ball so that the cat might or might not play with it.

On the sixth day, God created veterinary science to keep the cat healthy and the man broke.

On the seventh day, God tried to rest, but he had to scoop the litterbox.

— Unknown

The mysterious origin of cats

Over and over in cat histories I read that, in comparison to other animals, the cat was a very late arrival on the animal scene. Over and over in cat histories, too, I read such a sentence as "The early history of the cat is shrouded . . ." and then, not, as usually ends such sentences, "in antiquity" but rather, of all phrases, "in mystery."

As one now owned by a cat, I hardly found this surprising. So I irreverently wanted to ask, what else is new? One does not have to be cat-owned for long to know that, if there is one thing a cat loves better than anything else — save, possibly, making a large mess out of something which had been carefully arranged before he got there — it is a mystery.

And if he can, as he so often does, make a large mystery out of where he has been when you go to look for him, even though he was right there a moment ago, surely it must have been mother's milk for his ancestors to make a mystery out of where they originally came from.

— Cleveland Amory, *The Cat Who Came for Christmas*

CATS ARE GODS
(OR THINK THEY ARE)

Thou art the Great Cat, the avenger of the gods, and the judge of words, and the president of the sovereign chiefs and the governor of the holy Circle. Thou art indeed . . . the Great Cat.

— Inscription on the Royal Tombs at Thebes

In ancient times, cats were worshiped as gods. They have never forgotten this.

— Unknown

If God created man in his own image, you've got to wonder in whose image did he create the cat, a more noble creature?

— Unknown

Drew Schnoebelen
@Dschnoeb

Following

I bet Egyptians were all like "Yo, nobody in history will ever worship and revere cats like we do" and then came the internet.

A dog thinks . . .

"Hey, those people I live with feed me, love me, provide me with a nice, warm, dry house, pet me, and take good care of me. . . . *They must be gods!*"

A cat thinks . . .

"Hey, those people I live with feed me, love me, provide me with a nice, warm, dry house, pet me, and take good care of me. . . . *I must be a god!*"

— Unknown

Dogs believe they are human. Cats believe they are God.

— Jeff Valdez

TO CAT, OR NOT TO CAT:
THAT IS THE QUESTION

Should I get a job or just keep on buying lottery tickets? Should I get married or skip that battle? Should I have children or skip THAT battle? Should I have a scoop of ice cream or the whole container?

All of us, at points in our lives, face life-altering decisions like these.

But the most important of all: *Should I get a cat?*

We're sitting here having a chat
Stopping well shy of a spat:

    Could we or couldn't we? . . .

    Should we or shouldn't we? . . .

Why *wouldn't* we take in a cat?

— Robert Wilde

from The Onion

Common Benefits Of Cat Ownership

- Cats are adept at defending your home from mouse-sized robbers.

- Now you'll have something to do with your hands as you detail your diabolical schemes to a captured secret agent.

- Recent studies have shown that cat owners feel superior to others after being told of recent studies proving cat owners are superior to those around them.

- Adopting a cat means that those second-rate children's names you've been sitting on might finally be put to use.

- Taking care of a pet can teach children responsibility and never to leave the screen door open.

A home without a cat — and a well-fed, well-petted and properly revered cat — may be a perfect home, perhaps, but how can it prove title?

— Mark Twain

Every life should have nine cats.

— Unknown

REIGNING: CATS OR DOGS?

So, you've decided you want a pet. And after considering all the options — anacondas, hyenas, elk, rocks — you've narrowed it down to cats and dogs.

But which one? Which is smarter? Most affectionate? Least maintenance? Least likely to eat my shoes or puke on the rug?

Tough call.

Even the stupidest cat seems to know more than any dog.

— Eleanor Clark

If a dog jumps in your lap, it is because he is fond of you; but if a cat does the same thing, it is because your lap is warmer.

— Alfred North Whitehead

from Dave Barry

How to Deal with Subordinates

Remember the old saying: "A subordinate capable of thinking up an idea is a subordinate capable of realizing that there is no particular reason why he or she should be a subordinate, especially your subordinate." This is why dogs are so popular as pets. You can have a dog for its whole lifetime, and it will never once come up with a good idea. It will lie around for over a decade, licking its private parts and always reacting with total wonder and amazement to your ideas. "What!?" says the dog, when you call it to the door. "You want me to go *outside*!!? What a *great* idea!!! I never would have thought of that!!!"

Cats, on the other hand, don't think you're the least bit superior. They're always watching you with that smartass cat expression and thinking, "God, what a cementhead." Cats are always coming up with their own ideas. They are not team players, and they would make terrible corporate employees. A corporate department staffed by cats would be a real disciplinary nightmare, the kind of department that would never achieve 100 percent of its "fair share" pledge quota to the United Way. Dogs, on the other hand, would go way over the quota. Of course they'd also chew up the pledge cards.

The point I'm trying to make here, as far as I can tell, is that you want subordinates who, when it comes to thinking up ideas, are more like dogs than like cats.

— *Claw Your Way to the Top*

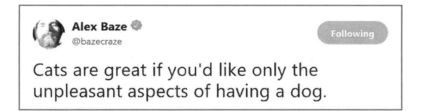

Cats are the ultimate narcissists. You can tell this because of all the time they spend on personal grooming. Dogs aren't like this. A dog's idea of personal grooming is to roll on a dead fish.

— James Gorman

Adopt a dog? Or a cat?

- If you want someone who will eat whatever you put in front of him and never say it's not as good as his mother's . . . then adopt a dog.

- If you want someone always willing to go out with you, at any hour, for as long and wherever you want . . . then adopt a dog.

- If you want someone who will never touch the remote, doesn't care about football, and can sit next to you as you watch romantic movies . . . then adopt a dog.

- If you want someone who is content to get on your bed just to warm your feet and whom you can push off if he snores . . . then adopt a dog.

- If you want someone who never criticizes what you do, doesn't care if you are pretty or ugly, fat or thin, young or old, who acts as if every word you say is especially worthy of his attention, and loves you unconditionally, perpetually . . . then adopt a dog.

- On the other hand, if you want someone who never responds when you call, ignores you when you come home, walks all over you, runs around all night and comes home only to eat and sleep, and acts as if your entire existence is solely to ensure his happiness . . . then adopt a cat.

— Unknown

Dogs come when they're called. Cats take a message and get back to you later.

— Mary Bly

from Jerome K. Jerome

Cats have the credit of being more worldly wise than dogs — of looking more after their own interests, and being less blindly devoted to those of their friends. And we men and women are naturally shocked at such selfishness. Cats certainly do love a family that has a carpet in the kitchen more than a family that has not; and if there are many children about, they prefer to spend their leisure time next door. But, taken altogether, cats are libeled. Make a friend of one, and she will stick to you through thick and thin. All the cats that I have had have been most firm comrades. I had a cat once that used to follow me about everywhere, until it even got quite embarrassing, and I had to beg her, as a personal favor, not to accompany me any further down the High Street. She used to sit up for me when I was late home, and meet me in the passage. It made me feel quite like a married man, except that she never asked where I had been, and then didn't believe me when I told her.

— *The Idle Thoughts of an Idle Fellow* (1890)

If animals could speak, the dog would be a blundering outspoken fellow; but the cat would have the rare grace of never saying a word too much.

— Mark Twain

The dog may be wonderful prose, but only the cat is poetry.

— French proverb

Every dog has his day — but the nights are reserved for cats.

— Unknown

To keep a proper perspective of one's own importance, everyone should have a dog who adores him and a cat who ignores him.

— Christian Bobin

When dogs leap onto your bed, it's because they adore being with you. When cats leap onto your bed, it's because they adore your bed.

— Alisha Everett

Dogs would make totally incompetent criminals. If you could somehow get a group of dogs to understand the concept of the Kennedy assassination, they would all immediately confess to it. Whereas you'll never see a cat display any kind of guilty behavior, despite the fact that several cats were seen in Dallas on the grassy knoll area, not that I wish to start rumors.

— Dave Barry

You own a dog; you feed a cat.

— Jim Fiebig

Dogs look up to you. Cats look down on you. Give me a pig. He just looks you in the eye and treats you like an equal.

— Winston Churchill

You call to a dog and a dog will break its neck to get to you. Dogs just want to please. Call to a cat and its attitude is, "What's in it for me?"

— Lewis Grizzard

monica heisey ✔
@monicaheisey

Following

and now it's time to play my cat's favourite game, What Happened In Here And Why Are You Wet?

Dogs seem more photogenic than cats. In photos most cats look like sociopaths.

— Demetri Martin

Cats will outsmart dogs every time.

— John Grogan

The cat's motto

No matter what you've done wrong, always try to make it look like the dog did it.

— Unknown

The truth about cats and dogs

What is a cat?

- Cats do what they want

- They rarely listen to you

- They're totally unpredictable

- They whine when they are not happy

- When you want to play, they want to be alone

- When you want to be alone, they want to play

- They expect you to cater to their every whim

- They're moody

- They leave hair everywhere

- They drive you nuts and cost you money

CONCLUSION: *Cats are tiny little women in fur coats.*

What is a dog?

- Dogs lie around all day, sprawled on the most comfortable piece of furniture in the house

- They can hear a package of food opening half a block away, but don't hear you when you're in the same room

- They can look dumb and lovable all at the same time

- They growl when they are not happy

- When you want to play, they want to play

- When you want to be alone, they want to play

- They are great at begging

- They will love you forever if you rub their tummies

- They can never have enough toys and they leave them everywhere

- They do disgusting things with their mouths and then they try to give you a kiss

CONCLUSION: *Dogs are tiny little men in fur coats.*

— Unknown

The cat is mightily dignified — until the dog comes along.

— Unknown

from Dave Barry

Cats are less loyal than dogs, but more independent. (This is code. It means: "Cats are smarter than dogs; but they hate people.") Many people love cats. From time to time, newspapers print stories about some elderly widow who died and left her entire estate, valued at $320,000, to her cat Fluffkins. Cats read these stories, too, and are always plotting to get named as beneficiaries in their owners' wills. Did you ever wonder where your cat goes when it wanders off for several hours? It meets with other cats in estate-planning seminars. I just thought you should know.

— *Dave Barry's Bad Habits*

Why cats are better than dogs

- Cats purr. Dogs drool.

- Cats rub your leg when they want affection, not when they're horny.

- Cats use a litter box. Dogs use your leg.

- Cats always land on their feet. Dogs just won't let you throw them.

- Cats will wait until you've read your morning paper before tearing it to shreds.

- Cats look cute sleeping on top of the TV. Dogs just crash right in front of the screen.

- Fewer cat owners suffer from "Flappy Tail" lacerations than dog owners.

- No one has ever had to "Beware of the Cat."

- Cats bury their crap. Dogs dig up others'.

- Cats have better things to do than stick their nose in your crotch.

- Cats lay themselves on the car in the heat. Dogs in heat lay the car.

- Why do you think they call it *dog breath*?

- Garfield. Odie. Enough said.

— Unknown

Why dogs are better than cats

- Dogs will tilt their heads and try to understand every word you say. Cats will ignore you and take a nap.

- Cats look silly on a leash.

- When you come home from work, your dog will be happy and lick your face. Cats will still be mad at you for leaving in the first place.

- Dogs will give you unconditional love until the day they die. Cats will make you pay for every mistake you've ever made since the day you were born.

- A dog knows when you're sad. And he'll try to comfort you. Cats don't care how you feel, as long as you remember where the can opener is.

- Dogs will bring you your slippers. Cats will drop a dead mouse in your slippers.

- When you take them for a ride, dogs will sit on the seat next to you. Cats need their own private basket or they won't go at all.

- Dogs will play fetch with you all day long. The only thing cats will play with all day long are small rodents or bugs, preferably ones that look like they're in pain.

- Dogs will wake you up if the house is on fire. Cats will quietly sneak out the back door.

— Unknown

Cats are smarter than dogs. You can't get eight cats to pull a sled through snow.

— Jeff Valdez

A dog is a man's best friend. A cat is a cat's best friend.

— Robert J. Vogel

A dog accepts you as the boss. A cat wants to see your resumé.

— Unknown

I don't see the purpose of cats. Dogs can protect you, can sniff out things, and can be your eyes if you're blind. Could you imagine a Seeing Eye cat? The first person who walks by with an untied shoelace, and you're history.

— Christine O'Rourke

A dog knows his master, a cat does not.

— Eleasar B. Zadok

Cats: I love them, they are so nice and selfish. Dogs are TOO good and unselfish. They make me feel uncomfortable. But cats are gloriously human.

— Lucy Maud Montgomery

A serious reason *not* to own a cat . . .

It might not get along with your snake.

— Dave Barry

The bottom line . . . get *something*

A house without either a cat or a dog is the house of a scoundrel.

— Portuguese proverb

SHOPPING FOR CATS

from The New Yorker

Pets Immediately Available for Adoption

Jason Roeder

Thank you for your interest in adopting a pet! While we can't guarantee that every dog or cat you see listed on our Web site will be available at the shelter when you arrive, there are several members of our furry family that have been with us quite a while and will almost certainly be here, eagerly awaiting you. Help give them the love they desperately, *desperately* need!

Jake

This three-year-old boxer mix suffered years of psychological abuse at the hands of his prior owners, in Brooklyn, who named him Terrence Q. Fluffernutter, Esq., for no discernible reason. Though he is slowly adjusting to having a real dog's name, Jake remains understandably skittish and could benefit from a less traumatically ironic environment.

Wanda

It's a mystery to us why this six-year-old calico has been here so long, other than the fact that she sits perfectly still all day — like, totally motionless. Never moves. This kitty would be perfect for any home that's looking for a low-maintenance pet or is seriously considering adopting a small pile of leaves.

Rufus

This terrier's face was badly wounded in a fight with a raccoon, but the disfigurement hasn't stopped anyone here from getting in lots of snuggles with him, provided that he is wearing the special balaclava that allows him to breathe but covers all exposed skin and bone. Rufus is best suited for a home that understands one simple rule: The special balaclava does not come off. The balaclava never comes off.

Coco

Here's one cocker spaniel that's great with kids — and only kids! While aggressive around adults, Coco would make a great companion for runaways or just children left at home unsupervised for weeks at a time.

Pepper

Somebody needs a tummy rub! But that somebody is not Pepper. A purrfect addition to any family, this five-year-old domestic shorthair is a cuddle machine! Except for his belly. Even approach his fluffy white tum-

tum, and he'll recoil and fix his eyes on you as if to say, "How dare you? Is there any trace of compassion inside you? Dostoevsky said that no animal could be as cruel as a man, and here you are, living testament to his word. You are the surest sign that if, *if*, God exists, he weeps for having made you in his image and for making me your mere toy."

Chloe

We will straight-up pay you five hundred dollars if you make Chloe disappear.

Boots

What if a cat was trained for dog-fighting but was subsequently forced into retirement because her bloodlust disturbed even her trainer? Come on down and meet Boots! We found this gray tabby gnawing straight through a tire three days ago. In the short time since then, every single one of us at the shelter has grown to fear and respect her! Boots probably isn't the best fit for a home with children in it — even visiting ones, even just in your doorway, trick-or-treating — and would be happiest in . . . we actually shudder to think what would make Boots happy. It may be best if the world never knows.

A pet store is a celebration of dogs' existence and an explosion of options. About cats, a pet store seems to say, "Here, we couldn't think of anything else." Cats are the Hanukkah of the animal world in this way. They are feted quietly and happily by a minority, but there's only so much hoopla applicable to them.

— Sloane Crosley

I got my dog three years ago because I was drunk in a pet store. We had nine cats at the time. The cats started hiding the alcohol after that.

— Paula Poundstone

KITTEN SMITTEN

If you do not want to have a cat, you must — at all costs — *steer clear of kittens*.

According to numerous cat owner surveys, fully 60% of all cat owners had zero intention of ever owning cats — until, by chance, they saw kittens. Then they had no chance.

Some say humans, especially female humans, are attracted to cats because cat faces look a lot like human baby faces. Maybe. We do know that the mere sight of kittens can melt the resolve of the hardest-headed, hardest-boiled of men. And women.

If we ever get serious about Middle East peace, someone should be sure that, in the room with the negotiators, there's a box of kittens.

It is impossible to keep a straight face in the presence of one or more kittens.

— Cynthia E. Varnado

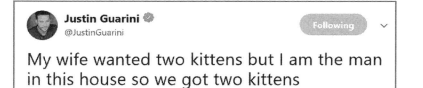

No matter how much cats fight, there always seem to be plenty of kittens.

— Attributed to Abraham Lincoln

The trouble with a kitten is that
Eventually it becomes a cat.

— Ogden Nash

What marvelous vitality a kitten has. It is really something very beautiful the way life bubbles over in the little creatures. They rush about, and mew, and spring; dance on their hind legs, embrace everything with their front ones, roll over and over, lie on their backs and kick. They don't know what to do with themselves, they are so full of life.

Can you remember, reader, when you and I felt something of the same sort of thing?

— Jerome K. Jerome, *The Idle Thoughts of An Idle Fellow* (1890)

How to Make a Kitten

Ed Page

I hope this article doesn't upset any cats. They've had a monopoly on kitten-making for as long as I can remember, so they may be a bit perturbed to learn that an outsider has figured out how to make one. But I've done just that. In fact, I've come up with a great many kitten-making techniques, one to suit every fancy, I daresay. Here, for instance, is a simple three-step method:

1. Find a full-grown cat.

2. Reverse the flow of time.

3. Wait.

I devised these procedures a few weeks ago in an all-night brainstorming session that arose when I mistook a couple of No-Doz for my sleeping pills. I sat out the night in my den, a cushiony chair beneath me, my beloved black kitten Debbie purring in my lap. As I sat there, puffing leisurely on my Basil Rathbone-style pipe, my mind wafted hither and yon. "How would one go about making a kitten?" I mused, gazing down at Debbie. "They're such complex little contraptions. So many moving parts!" I surprised myself with my ingenuity. Cogitating away in the wee hours, turning the question this way and that, I came up with a whole slew of solutions that now, in the light of day, strike me as flawless. (Loath to ignite Debbie's jealousy, I have yet to test any of them.) Below, I present a sampling of my solutions. Happy kitten-making!

The Vacuum Method

Using a standard vacuum cleaner or Dustbuster, suck up half the empty space from between the atoms that compose the body of an adult cat. Push the atoms together. Voilà! A kitten.

The Marionette Method

Carve a kitten marionette out of wood. Wish upon a star that it were a real live kitten. The Blue Fairy will eventually grant this wish, but not before the wooden kitten, brought magically to life, gets mixed up in many entertaining situations and is swallowed by a whale.

The Miracle Method

Travel back to the time when all the things in the New Testament were happening. Wangle an invitation to the water-into-wine party. After the wine miracle, approach Jesus with your goblet and explain that you're not much of a wine drinker and would rather have a kitten. Watch as Jesus performs the wine-into-kitten miracle.

The Costume Method

Wear a cat costume all day, every day. Never be seen not wearing the cat costume. When it comes time for you to have a baby, the stork will bring you a kitten.

The Dream Method

Fall asleep and dream that you have a kitten. Frolic with the kitten in a lush dream meadow full of wildflowers and happiness. When you feel yourself starting to wake up, grab the kitten and hold it gently but firmly close to your heart. When you're fully awake, look down at your arms; you're still holding the kitten!

The Giant House Method

Demolish your house. Rebuild it so it looks exactly the same, only twice as big. Fill the house with things that are twice the size they normally are: giant phones, giant chairs, giant toaster ovens, etc. Get a full-grown cat and put it in your house. What outside your house was a cat is now—

amazingly — a kitten. (Note: This method has the fun additional benefit of turning you into a dwarf.)

The Natural Method

Invite a handsome male cat and a pretty female cat over to your house for dinner. Light candles. Put on a Barry White CD. Serve your guests oyster-flavored Tender Vittles and plenty of wine. When you're sure both cats are drunk, escort them to the guest room. In the morning, after the cats have gone to their respective homes, strip the bed and plant the soiled sheets in your garden. Soon, a tree will start to grow. By late spring, the tree will be tall and leafy and full of kittens.

from The Onion

NEWS IN BRIEF

Middle-Aged Cat Can't Begin To Compete With Adorable Kittens On Internet

SARASOTA, FL — Lamenting that "some adorable, fluffy little bundle of fur and whiskers" seems to be in nearly every forwarded email and Facebook post nowadays, local middle-aged cat Rusty admitted to reporters today that he can't even begin to compete with the cute kittens from the internet. "Sure, people enjoy petting me when they first see me, and I can purr all night long, but put me next to a 15-second clip of a rambunctious little tabby pouncing on a toy and there's no way I can stack up," said the 7-year-old Maltese cat, who added that he didn't even want to think about how to contend with various tiny kitten memes, shareable images of kittens in a box, or startled-kitten animated .gifs. "Maybe if I were four or five years younger, my owner would take a video of me walking across the piano keyboard or arching my back and batting at my own reflection and I might make it big, but I'm too old for that now. The fact is, there are literally thousands of kittens online right now who are being more adorable than I could ever imagine, and that's something I just have to live with." After speaking with reporters, Rusty reportedly found himself contemplating whether he could win everyone's attention by videotaping himself running on his owner's treadmill, before gently reminding himself that "no, [his] time has passed."

NAME DAT CAT

We have two cats. They're my wife's cats, Mischa and Alex. You can tell a woman names a cat like this. Women always have sensitive names: Muffy, Fluffy, Buffy. Guys name cats things like Tuna Breath, Fur Face, Meow Head. They're nice cats. They've been neutered and they've been declawed. So they're like pillows that eat.

— Larry Reeb

I think cats would have an even worse attitude if they found out how stupid their names were.

— Demetri Martin

A cat's name may tell you more about its owners than it does about the cat.

— Linda W. Lewis

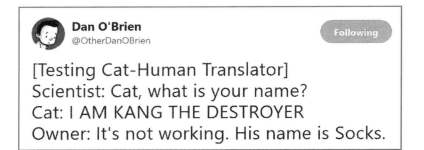

[Testing Cat-Human Translator]
Scientist: Cat, what is your name?
Cat: I AM KANG THE DESTROYER
Owner: It's not working. His name is Socks.

Giving the cat a name, like marriage, is not an easy thing. Soon I experienced the selection of name for a baby, a dog, a book, a warship, a sports team, even the king, the pope or a hurricane is just child's play compared to the selection of the cat's name.

— Cleveland Amory, *The Cat Who Came for Christmas*

from The Onion

NEWS IN BRIEF

All Of Pregnant Woman's Favorite Names Used Up On Cats

EUGENE, OR — Seven months pregnant with her first child, veteran cat lady Claudia Beck, 38, said Monday that she has already used all of her favorite names on her cats. "I've got Madison, Emily, Tyler, Jonathan, Claudia Jr., Dakota, and Todd," Beck said. "Then there's Smokey and Midnight, who are strays I feed." As of press time, Beck and the baby's father, animal-shelter assistant Rich Delgado, were considering naming their child "Boots."

Choosing your cat's name — mainstream or maniac?

Nala, Bella, Luna, Abby, Daisy . . . Simba, Milo, Tiger, Oreo, Bear. These are the five most popular names for female and male cats, according to a recent survey. Choose one of these names and you'll fit right in with the crowd.

Or you could try for something creative — like these:

- Chairman Meow
- Cat Middleton

- Anderson Pooper
- Fidel Catstro
- Catalie Portman
- Leonardo diCatrio
- Cindy Clawford
- Paw McCartney
- Katy Purry
- Bing Clawsby
- Ryan Fleacrest
- Frank Lloyd Bite
- Shakespurr
- The Great Catsby
- Walter Croncat

tara shoe
@tarashoe

Following

some cats are like "i hate this dumb name you gave me." but i like the ones that are clearly saying "FOOLS! COWER BEFORE THE IRE OF WAFFLES"

THAT MYSTERIOUS PERSONALITY

What goes on behind those deep, pools-of-mystery eyes?

Are cats secretly plotting to kill their owners and take over the household? (Nearly half of house cats have physically attacked their owners.)

Are cats pondering the many-worlds theory of quantum mechanics?

Are cats thinking of themselves as saber-tooth tigers — the rulers of all they survey, able to bring down mastodons and bison?

We know one thing for sure. Cats are spooked by sudden encounters with cucumbers and zucchinis. We know this from the many YouTube videos posted by cat owners who place a large cuke or zuke behind their unsuspecting cats. When the cats casually turn around and spot the dreaded object . . . let's just say that unless these cat owners had performed this helpful service, many of us may never have known the astonishing vertical height to which suddenly terrified cats can launch themselves.

Cats may have walnut-sized brains, but they have all the basic emotions we do — rage, anger, affection, curiosity, play, communication.

They just don't express their emotions that well. Then again, how well do we?

Who can believe that there is no soul behind those luminous eyes!

— Theophile Gautier

A cat is a puzzle for which there is no solution.

— Hazel Nicholson

Everything that moves serves to interest and amuse a cat. He is convinced that nature is busying herself with his diversion; he can conceive of no other purpose in the universe.

— F. A. Paradis de Moncrif

from The Onion

NEWS IN BRIEF

It Impossible To Tell What Sounds Will Freak Out Cat

DULUTH, MN — Saying that there seemed to be no clear pattern to the animal's responses, local pet owner Wendy Vogl reported Friday that it is impossible to tell what sounds will cause her cat to totally freak out. "I can slam the front door and he'll just sit there licking himself, but then he'll hear thunder and run out of the room immediately," said Vogl, adding that she could think of no rational explanation for why her cat, Max, would bolt the moment she switched on a hair dryer yet take the noise of a vacuum cleaner completely in stride. "If I had any clue at all what scared him, if there was any logic to it whatsoever, I could try not to do it as much. But I honestly think there's just no rhyme or reason for why my cat will totally lose his shit." At press time, Vogl had just plugged in her new food processor and had absolutely no idea if her cat would be hiding under the bed for the next three hours.

Cats have it all — admiration, an endless sleep, and company only when they want it.

— Rod McKuen

Just Gwen
@msgwenl

Following

I keep thinking my cats are sad about the election, but clearly I'm just projecting my own feelings because we all know cats are monarchists

I put down my book, *The Meaning of Zen*, and see the cat smiling into her fur as she delicately combs it with her rough pink tongue. "Cat, I would lend you this book to study but it appears you have already read it." She looks up and gives me her full gaze. "Don't be ridiculous" she purrs, "I wrote it."

— Dilys Laing, from "Miao"

The problem with cats is that they get the exact same look on their face whether they see a moth or an axe-murderer.

— Paula Poundstone

You cannot expect everything even from the friendliest cat. It is still a cat.

— Cleveland Amory, *The Cat Who Came for Christmas*

from The Onion

NEWS IN BRIEF

Cat Seemed Perfectly Content Right Up Until Point He Bolted Out Of Room

SOMERSET, NJ — Twenty-eight-year-old Jason Wagner confirmed Tuesday that his cat, Pepper, seemed totally relaxed and content up until the moment he jumped from the living room couch onto the floor and darted out of the living room. "For 15 minutes he was purring, sitting on my lap — asleep even — but, just like that, it all changed," Wagner said of his cat's abrupt, 180-degree mood shift. "One moment, you think he could lie there the entire day, and the next he's on some sort of impromptu search-and-destroy mission." At press time, Pepper had reportedly walked calmly back into the room, leapt onto the couch, and lain down as if nothing had happened.

The great question that has never been answered, and which I have not yet been able to answer, despite my thirty years of research into the feline soul, is "What does a cat want?"

— Sigmund Freud (with apologies)

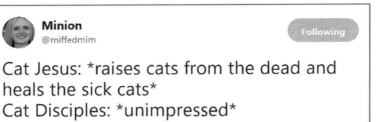

Cat Jesus: *raises cats from the dead and heals the sick cats*
Cat Disciples: *unimpressed*

If cats looked like frogs we'd realize what nasty, cruel little bastards they are. Style. That's what people remember.

— Terry Pratchett

I have cats because they have no artificially imposed, culturally prescribed sense of decorum. They live in the moment. If I had an aneurysm in the brain and dropped dead, I love knowing that, as the paramedics carry me out my cats are going to be swatting at that little toe tag.

— Paul Provenza

If you want to know what a tiger is like, look at a cat.

— Hindu proverb

Sixth Form Poet
@sixth_formpoet

It's so sad that curiosity led to so many life-changing inventions, but is still mostly remembered for killing that one cat.

Cat: A pygmy lion who loves mice, hates dogs, and patronizes human beings.

— Oliver Herford

A cat can climb down from a tree without the assistance of the fire department or any other agency. The proof is that no one has ever seen a cat skeleton in a tree.

— Unknown

Do not meddle in the affairs of cats, for they are subtle and will piss on your computer.

— Bruce Graham

from The Onion

NEWS IN BRIEF

Cat Internally Debates Whether Or Not To Rip Head Off Smaller Creature It Just Met

ROCKVILLE, MD — Staring attentively at the potential prey while carefully weighing its best course of action, local cat Jasper was reportedly locked in an intense internal debate Wednesday about whether or not to rip the head off a smaller creature it had just happened upon. "Hmm, should I just walk on by or should I sink my teeth into its neck and pop that little head right off?" the 6-year-old American shorthair reportedly thought to itself, prowling within striking distance as it mulled over viciously decapitating the seemingly unaware chipmunk that stood foraging in the grass just a few feet away from it or simply continuing on with its day. "I could pounce on that thing and snap its head off in one bite, easy. Or I could just slink over there and curl up on that chair on the deck. Tough call." At press time, the cat had opted to bat around the mortally wounded rodent a few dozen times to give it a little extra time to decide.

The cat's a saint when there are no mice about.

— Japanese proverb

WHEN CATS ARE SAD

Bartender: What'll ya have?
Cat: Shot of rum.
[Bartender pours it]
[Cat slowly pushes it off the bar]
Cat: Another.

A cat is more intelligent than people believe, and can be taught any crime.

— Mark Twain

Cats don't like change without their consent.

— Roger A. Caras

Cats are connoisseurs of comfort.

— James Herriot

Some people say that cats are sneaky, evil, and cruel. True, and they have many other fine qualities as well.

— Missy Dizick

Cats are notoriously sore losers. Coming in second best, especially to someone as poorly coordinated as a human being, grates their sensibility.

— Stephen Baker

Authors like cats because they are such quiet, lovable, wise creatures, and cats like authors for the same reasons.

— Robertson Davies

Recently we were discussing the possibility of making one of our cats Pope, and we decided that the fact that she was not Italian, and was female, made the third point, that she was a cat, irrelevant.

— Katharine Whitehorn

Cats never feel threatened. They are genetically incapable of accepting that anyone could possibly dislike anything as perfect as a cat.

— Kathy Young

A man has to work so hard so that something of his personality stays alive. A tomcat has it so easy, he has only to spray and his presence is there for years on rainy days.

— Albert Einstein

Most cats, when they are Out want to be In, and vice versa, and often simultaneously.

— Louis J. Camuti

Some people say man is the most dangerous animal on the planet. Obviously those people have never met an angry cat.

— Lillian Johnson

Cats seem to go on the principle that it never does any harm to ask for what you want.

— Joseph Wood Krutch

The trouble with cats is that they've got no tact.

— P.G. Wodehouse

One cat just leads to another.

— Ernest Hemingway

Cats' hearing apparatus is built to allow the human voice to easily go in one ear and out the other.

— Stephen Baker

Never try to out-stubborn a cat.

— Lazarus Long

Chris Priestly
@TheEvilChris

Following ⌄

Lets plant catnip, he said. It prevents mosquitoes, he said. What could go wrong, he said. #cats

Cats are rather delicate creatures and they are subject to a good many ailments, but I never heard of one who suffered from insomnia.

— Joseph Wood Krutch

There is no snooze button on a cat who wants breakfast.

— Unknown

Cats always know whether people like or dislike them. They do not always care enough to do anything about it.

— Winifred Carriere

It's very hard to be polite if you're a cat.

— Unknown

from The Onion

NEWS IN BRIEF

House Cat Announces Plans To Just Sit There For 46 Minutes

PARSIPPANY, NJ — Addressing reporters from the living room floor Wednesday, local house cat Tabitha announced her plans to sit completely motionless in the same spot for the next 46 minutes. "After carefully considering my options, I have decided to sit down right here and not move for the next three quarters of an hour," the American shorthair informed reporters, adding that she intended to stare directly forward for the majority of the period. "Of course, I'm not ruling out any potential minor adjustments to this plan. I might, for instance, momentarily break from this position to stretch, roll onto my side, lick myself, or crane my neck into the path of a sunbeam, after which I will promptly return to my current arrangement. One thing is certain, however: Precisely 46 minutes from now, apropos of absolutely nothing, I will leap from my seated position and bolt out of the room, as if responding to an urgent matter that needs my attention. That I can assure you." At press time, Tabitha was forced to radically alter her agenda and make an immediate exit when her owner entered the living room and attempted to show affection toward her.

If the claws didn't retract, cats would be like Velcro.

— Bruce Fogle

Allergic to cat stare?

I love the way my cats stare at me. It's this long, penetrating, accusing glare like they've got some dirt on me. "I know you steal from work; I've seen the pens with the company name on them. Here are my demands. Fancy Feast only; no store brands, or I'm on the phone to management."

— Andi Rhoads

Surely the cat, when it assumes the meat loaf position and gazes meditatively through slitted eyes, is pondering thoughts of utter profundity.

— Mij Colson Barnum

Cats always seem so very wise, when staring with their half-closed eyes. Can they be thinking, "I'll be nice, and maybe she will feed me twice?"

— Bette Midler

from The Onion

NEWS IN BRIEF

Cat Looking Out Window, Bird Form Unbelievably Intense Fifth-Of-A-Second Bond

ADRIAN, MI — An extremely intense bond that lasted just 0.2 seconds, but which was filled with a range of deeply intertwined and conflicting emotions that included fear, hunger, curiosity, rage, and even — on some level — love, was reportedly felt Monday between Lionel, a tabby housecat, and a pine warbler. The brief, silent connection, described to reporters as an overwhelming, almost spiritual experience for both animals, almost as if everything in their short lives had been cosmically leading up to this very encounter, formed when Lionel, seated in his usual spot near the kitchen window, instinctually moved his head rapidly to the left and spotted the bird coming to rest on the patio table. During the milliseconds the two species locked eyes, age-old genetic impulses of survival were reportedly unlocked and the two animals were suddenly frozen in time, enveloped by the most primal and elemental forces of nature. According to witness accounts, at the height of their ever-so-short but fathomless bond, the cat and bird truly believed they were the only two living things in the entire universe, gripped by an almost paralyzing sense of yearning. The unexplained connection, which sources confirmed was as awesome, mighty, and holy as God Himself, ended as soon as it

began when the warbler flew away and Lionel scratched his ear and lay
down.

Are cats lazy? Well, more power to them if they are. Which one of us has
not entertained the dream of doing just as he likes, when and how he
likes, and as much as he likes?

— Fernand Mery

Cats can be very funny, and have the oddest ways of showing they're glad
to see you. Rudimac always peed in our shoes

— W.H. Auden

If you try and take a cat apart to see how it works, the first thing you have
on your hands is a non-working cat.

— Douglas Adams

If stretching meant wealth, the cat would be rich.

— Unknown

My cat violates a vital code
when she sleeps on the lid of my commode.
It is all right for her to choose it —
except, of course, when I have to use it.
It seems to me a cat should know
when you gotta go, you gotta go.
I'm sure she also would be bitter
if I slept in her box of litter.

— John D. Engle, Jr.

The great charm of cats is their rampant egotism, their devil-may-care attitude toward responsibility, their disinclination to earn an honest dollar.

— Robertson Davies

The cat could very well be man's best friend but would never stoop to admitting it.

— Doug Larson

Ah, the catnap . . .

One of the ways in which cats show happiness is by sleeping.

— Cleveland Amory, *The Cat Who Came for Christmas*

The cat sleeps on the sheik's lap and is at home on the prayer carpet.

— Attar of Nishapur (1145–1221)

Kittens are born with their eyes shut. They open them in about six days, take a look around, then close them again for the better part of their lives.

— Stephen Baker

The mystery of the nine lives

Do radioactive cats have eighteen half-lives?

— Steven Wright

I bought a generic cat. It only had five lives.

— Matt Wohlfarth

- yet more proof that cats are in fact a kind of liquid

A cat will assume the shape of its container.

— Unknown

Rain. The bane of every self-respecting cat.

You have no idea how devastating it is to the pelt of the cat and its self-worth. Rain makes the cat ugly. His pelt was meant to be gorgeous, to be admired in full feline splendor. A wet pelt, however, shows the cat underneath, the thin rat-like tail, the thin pathetic body with the ugly big head. No cat worthy of calling himself Feline Finest should ever be seen when wet. With the dignity goes the serenity and good temper. A wet cat must dry himself as fast as possible and in the meantime any human witnessing his shame will have to fear Feline Wrath. Don't ever laugh at your dripping cat.

— Babeth van Son, *Tales from the House of Chaos*

Happiness is like a cat. If you try to coax it or call it, it will avoid you. It will never come. But if you pay no attention to it and go about your business, you'll find it rubbing up against your legs and jumping into your lap.

— William Bennett

If there is one spot of sun spilling onto the floor, a cat will find it and soak it up.

— Joan Asper McIntosh

from The Onion

NEWS

Cat Congress Mired In Sunbeam

WASHINGTON, D.C. — The current session of the 111th Cat Congress was once again suspended Tuesday following the sudden introduction of a sunbeam onto the Senate floor, a development that has left a majority of transfixed lawmakers unable to move forward.

The ray of sunlight, which first appears in the official record at 11:30 a.m., interrupted debate over S. 391, a proposal to provide underprivileged felines with universal access to scratching posts.

"We've come up against an unforeseen circumstance, but we'll resume deliberation and voting as quickly as is reasonably possible," said majority leader and Budget Committee chaircat Sen. Creamsicle (D-ND), stretching out to his entire length and repeatedly kneading the chamber carpet. "I think I speak for most of my colleagues when I say that, while it is extremely important we continue the legislative work at hand, we must first give this warm and bright beam of light the due consideration it deserves."

"And we should, er, debate this for as long as it takes," added Creamsicle, softly swishing his tail back and forth. "Perhaps all day, if we have to."

A majority of senators seemed to agree with Creamsicle. Eighty-nine of the 100 congresscats present immediately joined the new Sunbeam Investigative Committee, and a number of subcommittees are also reported to have been created, the largest of which has been tasked with determining the value of lazily batting at rising dust motes while half-asleep.

A small minority of feline senators, however, took issue with the procedural delay. Sen. Poppy (D-DE) was especially vocal, claiming that the Senate should ignore the seemingly intractable sunbeam issue and continue with other, more pressing matters.

"This irresponsible stoppage is absolutely unacceptable," Poppy said. "Frivolous distractions like these are robbing our constituents of the soft, cozy shafts of . . . I mean, the reforms they so desperately need . . . so desperately need. . . . I yield my remaining time."

Some legislators refused to participate in the debate altogether, most notably Sen. Ruby (R-SC), who spent several hours sitting motionless in front of the northwest wall of the Cat Capitol Building, staring unblinkingly at an unknown object.

The sunbeam marked the fourth event to suspend congressional activity this week. According to sources, other disruptions included a thunderclap on Monday that instantly adjourned proceedings; Wednesday's chaotic introduction of a laser pointer; and the discovery of a large cardboard box in the Capitol Rotunda Thursday that prompted minority whip Sen. Tiddles (R-TN) to call a recess so that he could sit inside of it.

None of these delays, however, compares to the appearance of a small sparrow outside the congressional chamber last month, which completely mesmerized House Speaker Jeffy-Boy (D-CA) and brought all government activity to a standstill for approximately 17 minutes.

Big Stripey, founder of the influential political watchdog committee litter.com, said he isn't surprised by the latest sunbeam debacle, claiming that years of corruption and mating scandals have shown just how ineffectual the current Cat Congress really is.

"Our lawmakers were elected to serve the common cat, not their own self-interests," Big Stripey said. "With over 6 percent of the population stray, millions more going hungry or only getting dry food, and the dogs next door developing a very real litter of puppies, we need action now for the sake of our kittens and our kittens' kittens."

"We're not paying these idiots to sit around and lick each other all day," Big Stripey added.

Many congressional insiders refuted accusations of indolence, saying that the rigorous schedule of cat legislators entitles them to periodic breaks in addition to their 18 scheduled hours of sleep per day.

"Our Founding Toms understood that certain provisions must be made in the interest of the public good," congressional spokescat Georgina said. "Democracy is not always so cut and dried. Sunbeams are going to happen. Vacuum cleaners are going to happen. Those little springy wires with a piece of cardboard at the end are going to happen. It's simply the way the system works."

According to late reports, the Cat Congress had briefly reconvened due to cloudy weather, but was quickly adjourned again after a crumpled up piece of aluminum foil suddenly rolled across the Senate floor.

Fillet of Sol

The sun slants in, its light a wedge
Of carpet by the door.
And to that slice of sunlight
Goes my cat, now, to restore
Herself. This nap is therapeutic
(Like the tuna she devoured).
She seems to need this daily bask.
She thinks she's solar powered.

— Lee Anny Wynn Snook

Lettin' the cat outta the bag is a whole lot easier 'n puttin' it back in.

— Will Rogers

HOW To CARE FOR YOUR CAT

Now that you've acquired a cat and have committed to a till-death-do-us-part relationship, you need to know how to raise it properly — how to keep it healthy and happy.

Don't assume this will "come naturally." It doesn't, any more than raising children. You know the disasters that happen when parents don't raise their children properly — you see them every day in the people all around you.

Don't let this to happen to your cats.

Remember: If your cat is not purring continuously, you're failing.

from The Onion

Tips For Spoiling Your Cat

- Throw in a few extra brushing sessions on top of the required 25 per day.

- Double your daily calorie intake to expand the width of your lap.

- You don't need a special occasion to treat them to an empty cardboard box in the middle of the week!

- Indulge your pet by setting aside an area of the house that's just for him, such as your bed or laptop keyboard.

- Give your cat an extra-special treat by devoting an entire day to leaving him alone.

Raising cats

Like children, cats don't come with instruction manuals.

But nowadays just about every community college offers affordable courses in cat parenting. Typical lessons include "From Power Struggles to Encouragement," "Challenges in Discipline," "Using Time Outs Effectively," "Repairing Furniture Scratches," "Armor for Cat Baths,"

"Hearing Protection for a Good Night's Sleep," "No, You Don't Need to Call the Fire Department," and more.

Before you know it — time does fly — you'll need to sit down with your cat or cats and have that talk. Don't assume your cat trainer will take care of this. Heaven forbid their only source of information is their friends and the Internet.

As much as you wish your cats would abstain until they've found that special someone, that serious, long-term relationship, you can assume your cats are going to be sexually active.

Do your best to help your cats appreciate the enduring value of love. Help them see how true love can turn sex, late at night beneath the dumpster, into something truly beautiful and life-affirming.

At least caution your cats always to use protection. In their passion, they may assume "it won't happen to me." But cat sex frequently does lead to kittens. Help your cats understand they may not be mature enough to care for kittens, also that kittens can derail their plans for college and a career.

You could have them neutered, yes. But ponder the moral dimensions. Would you inflict such procedures on your own children, without their consent? Would you deny your children — or your cats — the amazing fulfillment of children or kittens of their own?

A quick note on catnip: True, catnip is now legal in all states — but caution your cats about moderation. Today's catnip is not your grandmother's catnip.

Above all, give your cats the best education you can. Your cats will need top grades, starting in purr-school and kittengarden. It will be stressful, possibly traumatizing. But only with perfect 800s on their CATs will your cats stand a chance of getting into a *US Mews* top-ten school, and from there into claw school.

With degrees in paw, your cats will be on their way to lucrative catsulting jobs on Ball Street, to Catillac luxury coupes, homes in Westcheshire, and pairings with 1% cats that will cement their fat cat status. Well on their way, in other words, to happiness.

And then they'll be able to take care of you in your old age — if they haven't totally forgotten about you.

— Robert Wilde

How To Raise some cats

I is good to know how to take care of cats. First get some cats because you couldn't do it without cats. Next feed them and give them water every day or they well die. Then scoop poop or it well stink to high heaven. But no matter what you should always love them.

by wyatt   Mar 2003

FEEDING YOUR CAT

> **mark**
> @TheCatWhisprer
>
> *Following*
>
> Rachel Ray now makes cat food with real beef just like the cows my cat would eat in the wild.

Why isn't there mouse-flavored cat food?

— George Carlin

Usually I know exactly what the cat has eaten. Not only have I fed it to the cat, at the cat's insistence, but the cat has thrown it up on the rug and someone has tracked it all the way over onto the other rug. I don't know why cats are such habitual vomiters. They don't seem to enjoy it, judging by the sounds they make while doing it. Every so often cats say to themselves, "Well, time to vomit," and then they do. It's their nature. A dog is going to bark, a cat is going to vomit.

If I offend you, I'm sorry. But these problems exist. It is no good sweeping cat vomit under the rug.

— Roy Blount, Jr., *Not Exactly What I Had In Mind*

I bought a bird feeder. It was expensive, but I figured in the long run it would save me money on cat food.

— Linda Herskovic

from McSweeney's

On the care and feeding of cats

Teddy Wayne

A scalded cat fears cold water — and don't even *think* about putting Mr. Fluffers into a lukewarm bath, because he'll claw your face. Make sure to feed him twice a day, but alternate the cans; morning's on the left cabinet, night's on the right. My right. Yes. Here's his eye drops — each night, you'll have to hold him down without being, like, aggressive about it, or he'll claw your face, and dispense six drops into each eye or else he's vulnerable to pink eye. If he gets it, you'll basically catch it, too. He wakes up around five, five-thirty, and will start meowing and jumping on the bed and clawing your face, but after you feed him, you can go back to bed, and he won't claw you again till six-thirty, six at the earliest. What else . . . I think that's it! If there's an emergency, just call us in Thailand anytime using your own phone. No, we don't trim his nails here.

— *Teddy Wayne's Unpopular Proverbs*

The clever cat eats cheese and breathes down rat holes with baited breath.

— W.C. Fields

The Cat Miracle Diet

Most diets fail because we are still thinking and eating like people. For those us who have never had any success dieting, now there is the new Cat Miracle Diet!

Most cats are long and lean (or tiny and petite). The Cat Miracle Diet will help you achieve the same lean, svelte figure. Just follow this diet for 4 days and you'll find that you not only look and feel better, but you will have a whole new outlook on what constitutes food. Good Luck!

DAY 1

Breakfast — Open can of expensive gourmet cat food. Any flavor as long as it cost more than $0.75 per can — and place 1/4 cup on your plate. Eat 1 bite of food; look around room disdainfully. Knock the rest on the floor. Stare at the wall for awhile before stalking off into the other room.

Lunch — Four blades of grass and one lizard tail. Throw it back up on the cleanest carpet in your house.

Dinner — Catch a moth and play with it until it is almost dead. Eat one wing. Leave the rest to die.

Bedtime snack — Steal one green bean from your spouse's or partner's plate. Bat it around the floor until it goes under the refrigerator. Steal one small piece of chicken and eat half of it. Leave the other half on the sofa.

Throw out the remaining gourmet cat food from the can you opened this morning.

DAY 2

Breakfast — Pick up the remaining chicken bite from the sofa. Knock it onto the carpet and bat it under the television set. Chew on the corner of the newspaper as your spouse/partner tries to read it.

Lunch — Break into the fresh French bread that you bought as your part of the dinner party on Saturday. Lick the top of it all over. Take one bite out of the middle of the loaf.

Afternoon snack — Catch a large beetle and bring it into the house. Play toss and catch with it until it is mushy and half dead. Allow it to escape under the bed.

Dinner — Open a fresh can of dark-colored gourmet cat food — tuna or beef works well. Eat it voraciously. Walk from your kitchen to the edge of the living room rug. Promptly throw up on the rug. Step into it as you leave. Track footprints across the entire room.

DAY 3

Breakfast — Drink part of the milk from your spouse's or partner's cereal bowl when no one is looking. Splatter part of it on the closest polished aluminum appliance you can find.

Lunch — Catch a small bird and bring it into the house. Play with it on top of your down-filled comforter. Make sure the bird is seriously injured but not dead before you abandon it for someone else to have to deal with.

Dinner — Beg and cry until you are given some ice cream or milk in a bowl of your own. Take three licks/laps, and then turn the bowl over on the floor.

FINAL DAY

Breakfast — Eat six bugs, any type, being sure to leave a collection of legs, wings, and antennae on the bathroom floor. Drink lots of water. Throw up the bugs and all the water on your spouse's or partner's pillow.

Lunch — Remove the chicken skin from last night's chicken-to-go leftovers your spouse or partner placed in the trash can. Drag the skin across the floor several times. Chew on it in a corner and then abandon.

Dinner — Open another can of expensive gourmet cat food. Select a flavor that is especially runny, like Chicken and Giblets in Gravy. Lick off all the gravy and leave the actual meat to dry and get hard.

— Unknown

CAT HAIKU
PART 1

You never feed me.
Perhaps I'll sleep on your face.
That will show you.

You must scratch me there!
Yes, above my tail! Behold,
elevator butt.

I need a new toy.
Tail of black dog keeps good time.
Pounce! good dog! good dog!

The rule for today.
Touch my tail, I shred your hand.
New rule tomorrow.

In deep sleep hear sound
Cat vomit hairball somewhere.
Will find in morning.

Grace personified
I leap into the window
I meant to do that.

Blur of motion, then —
Silence, me, a paper bag
What is so funny?

The mighty hunter
Returns with gifts of plump birds
Your foot just squashed one.

You're always typing
Well, let's see you ignore my
Sitting on your hands.

My small cardboard box
You cannot see me if I
Can just hide my head.

Terrible battle
I fought for hours. Come and see!
What's a "term paper"?

Kitty likes plastic
Confuses for litter box
Don't leave tarp around.

Small brave carnivores
Kill pine cones and mosquitoes
Fear vacuum cleaner.

Want to trim my claws
Don't even think about it!
My yelps will wake the dead.

I want to be close
To you. Can I fit my head
inside your armpit?

Wanna go outside.
Oh, no! Help! I got outside!
Let me back inside!

Oh no! Big One
has been trapped by newspaper.
Cat to the rescue!

Humans are so strange.
Mine lies still in the bed, then screams!
My claws aren't that sharp . . . .

Cats meow out of angst
"Thumbs! If only we had thumbs!
We could break so much."

Litter box not there
You must have moved it again
I'll crap in the sink.

The Big Ones snore now
Every room is dark and cold
time for "Cup Hockey."

We're almost equals
I purr to show I love you
Want to smell my butt?

— Unknown

FRETTING THE VET

My apartment is the entire world to my indoor cat. Going to the vet is like visiting a galactic hub with strange creatures everywhere.

— Unknown

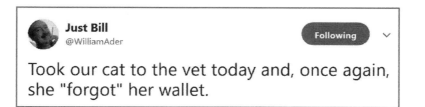

from The Onion

Tips For Choosing The Right Veterinarian

Bringing a pet into your life is a rewarding experience, though it also involves finding someone you trust to provide capable medical care. Here are *The Onion's* tips for choosing the right veterinarian:

- Begin by scoping out the facilities. If the vet's clinic has several heavy, padlocked doors that say "KEEP OUT," you can rest assured that they value your pet's privacy.

- Do your research to ensure the facility is open during the hours when your pet typically swallows an entire tube of tennis balls.

- Look for red flags around the office, such as unsanitary bathrooms and piles of dead horses.

- Make sure the vet demonstrates a keen interest in your pet. If they spend most of the appointment asking about your skin, this could indicate you've entered a dermatologist's office.

- Before letting the veterinarian work on your beloved turtle, give them a decoy turtle to prove themselves first.

- Be certain that the vet is passionate about animals and didn't just attend a college of veterinary medicine to make a quick buck.

- Not all clinics welcome walk-ins. If you're seeking off-the-books treatment for a gunshot wound, be sure to call ahead.

- If the search for the right specialist is too difficult, simply set your dog loose equidistant from all the vets in town to see where their instincts guide them.

- It's important to note the office's proximity to an ice cream parlor in the event that you have to soothe a sobbing child.

How to give your cat a pill

There are all sorts of occasions when you may need to give your cat pills — nutritional supplements, medications, tapeworm de-wormers, flea infestation control, anxiety relievers (particularly when they're studying for their CATs), NoDoz (particularly when they're studying for their CATs), and more.

But swallowing pills does not come naturally to cats. Here is the time-tested method.

- Pick up cat and cradle it in the crook of your left arm as if holding a baby. The trick is to be calm and confident.

- Position right forefinger and thumb on either side of cat's mouth and gently apply pressure to cheeks while holding pill in right hand. As cat opens mouth, pop pill into mouth. Allow cat to close mouth and swallow. Notice the direction the cat runs as it goes berserk.

- Retrieve pill from floor and cat from under sofa. Put on long sleeves. Cradle cat in left arm and repeat process. The trick is to remain calm and confident.

- Retrieve soggy pill and throw it away. Retrieve cat from behind dresser in bedroom.

- Get new pill, cradle cat in left arm, holding rear legs tightly with left hand. Force jaws open and push pill to back of mouth with right forefinger. Hold mouth shut for a count of ten, or until you lose control. Take note of direction it runs as you grab some Band-Aids for your arm.

- Retrieve pill from floor and cat from top shelf in closet. Call spouse to help.

- Kneel on floor with cat wedged firmly between knees, hold front and rear legs. Ignore low growls emitted by cat. Get spouse to hold head firmly with one hand while forcing wooden ruler into mouth. Drop pill down ruler and rub cat's throat vigorously.

- Get another pill and retrieve cat, which will be clinging to top of curtains. Make note to buy new ruler and repair curtains. Collect shattered objects and set aside for gluing later.

- Wrap cat in large towel and get spouse to firmly hold cat with head just visible. Put pill in end of drinking straw, force mouth open with pencil, and blow down drinking straw.

- Check label to make sure pill not harmful to humans; beer is effective to take taste away. Apply bandages as needed to spouse's arms and clean blood from carpet with cold water and soap before it sets.

- Retrieve cat from neighbor's garage. Get another pill. Open another beer. Place cat in cupboard, and close door gently onto neck, to leave head showing. Force mouth open with dessert spoon. Flick pill down throat with rubber band.

- Find screwdriver and put cupboard door back on hinges. Drink two shots of Scotch. Apply antiseptic to cheek, and ice to control swelling. Check records for date of last tetanus shot. Throw shredded shirt away and fetch new one.

- Call fire department to retrieve cat from tree. Offer to reimburse neighbor who hit fence while swerving to avoid cat.

- Get new pill; find heavy-duty pruning gloves from shed. Tie all four of cat's legs together with garden twine and bind tightly to leg of dining table. Open cat's mouth with pliers and push pill into mouth followed by large piece of wild-caught gourmet salmon. Hold head vertically and pour one cup of water down throat to wash pill down. Take note of direction cat runs with attached table leg.

- Consume remainder of Scotch. Get spouse to drive you to the emergency room, be patient while doctor stitches fingers and forearm and removes pill remnants from right eye. Call furniture shop on way home to order new table.

- Concede defeat. Arrange for SPCA to collect zombie mutant cat from hell when it returns three days later. Stop by pet shop and buy a gerbil.

— Unknown

from The Onion

NEWS IN BRIEF

Pet Owner Not Bothering To Neuter Loser Cat

CORAL SPRINGS, FL — Mike Oakland, 29, told reporters Monday he is not about to pay $100 to have his 5-month-old cat, Mowgli, neutered, because he has no expectations that the dull, paunchy tabby will ever get laid.

"For all he's going to use those balls, he might as well keep them," said Oakland, adding that he'd bet anyone any amount of money that the striped kitten will die a virgin. "He never leaves the house, and I've seen how the neighbor cat looks at him. Completely platonic." When reached for comment, a spokesperson from the Florida Humane Society reiterated that it's important to have all pets spayed or neutered, even ugly lame-o's who probably couldn't score in a roomful of calicos in heat.

BATHING YOUR CAT

The only self-cleaning thing in this house is the cat.

— Refrigerator magnet

Cats are among the cleanest animals in the world, if you set aside their being covered with their own spit.

— Unknown

I gave my cat a bath the other day; they love it. He enjoyed it, it was fun for me. The fur would stick to my tongue, but other than that . . .

— Steve Martin

Anybody who doesn't know what soap tastes like never washed a cat.

— Franklin P. Jones

from The Dog

How to wash the cat

- Thoroughly clean the toilet (this step is optional, as you'll see later).

- Add the required amount of shampoo to the toilet water, and have both lids lifted.

- Obtain the cat and soothe him while you carry him towards the bathroom.

- In one smooth movement, put the cat in the toilet and close both lids. You may need to stand on the lid so that he cannot escape. CAUTION: Do not get any part of your body too close to the edge, as his paws will be reaching out for any purchase they can find.

- Flush the toilet three or four times. This provides a "power wash and rinse" which has been found to be quite effective.

- Have someone open the door to the outside and ensure there are no people between the toilet and the outside door.

- Stand behind the toilet as far as you can, and quickly lift both lids.

- The now-clean cat will rocket out of the toilet and run outside where he will dry himself. Both the cat *and* the toilet will be sparkling clean!

Cat Bathing as a Martial Art

Bud Herron

Some people say cats never have to be bathed. They say cats lick themselves clean. They say cats have a special enzyme of some sort in their saliva that works like new, improved Wisk — dislodging the dirt where it hides and whisking it away.

I've spent most of my life believing this folklore. Like most blind believers, I've been able to discount all the facts to the contrary — the kitty odors that lurk in the corners of the garage and dirt smudges that cling to the throw rug by the fireplace.

The time comes, however, when a man must face reality: when he must look squarely in the face of massive public sentiment to the contrary and announce: "This cat smells like a port-a-potty on a hot day in Juarez."

When that day arrives at your house, as it has in mine, I have some advice you might consider as you place your feline friend under your arm and head for the bathtub:

- Know that although the cat has the advantages of quickness and utter disregard for human life, you have the advantage of strength. Capitalize on that advantage by selecting the battlefield. Don't try to bathe him in an open area where he can force you to chase him. Pick a very small bathroom. If your bathroom is more than four feet square, I recommend that you get in the tub with the cat and close the sliding-glass doors as if you were about to take a shower. (A simple shower curtain will not do. A berserk cat can shred a three-ply rubber shower curtain quicker than a politician can shift positions.)

- Know that a cat has claws and will not hesitate to remove all the skin from your body. Your advantage here is that you are smart and know how to dress to protect yourself. I recommend canvas overalls tucked into high-top construction boots, a pair of steel-mesh gloves, an army helmet, a hockey face mask and a long-sleeve flak jacket.

- Prepare everything in advance. There is no time to go out for a towel when you have a cat digging a hole in your flak jacket. Draw the water. Make sure the bottle of kitty shampoo is inside the glass enclosure. Make sure the towel can be reached, even if you are lying on your back in the water.

- Use the element of surprise. Pick up your cat nonchalantly, as if to simply carry him to his supper dish. (Cats will not usually notice your strange attire. They have little or no interest in fashion as a rule. If he does notice your garb, calmly explain that you are taking part in a product-testing experiment for J.C. Penney).

- Once you are inside the bathroom, speed is essential to your survival. In a single, fluid motion, shut the bathroom door, step into the tub enclosure, slide the glass door shut, dip the cat in the water and squirt him with shampoo. You have begun one of the wildest 45 seconds of your life.

- Cats have no handles. Add the fact that he now has soapy fur, and the problem is radically compounded. Do not expect to hold on to him for more that two or three seconds at a time. When you have him, however, you must remember to give him another squirt of shampoo and rub like crazy. He'll then spring free and fall back into the water, thereby rinsing himself off (the national record is — for cats — three latherings, so don't expect too much).

- Next, the cat must be dried. Novice cat bathers always assume this part will be the most difficult, for humans generally are worn out at this point and the cat is just getting really determined. In fact, the drying is simple compared to what you have just been through. That's because by now the cat is semi-permanently affixed to your right leg. You simply pop the drain plug with your foot, reach for your towel and wait. (Occasionally, however, the cat will end up clinging to the top of your army helmet. If this happens, the best thing you can do is shake him loose and encourage him toward your leg). After all the water is drained from the tub, it is a simple matter just to reach down and dry the cat.

- Do NOT try to use a blow dryer. You might as well use a vacuum cleaner.

In a few days the cat will relax enough to be removed from your leg. He will usually have nothing to say for about three weeks and will spend a lot of time sitting with his back to you. He might even become psycho-ceramic and develop the fixed stare of a plaster figurine.

You will be tempted to assume he is angry. This isn't usually the case. As a rule he is simply plotting ways to get through your defenses and injure you for life the next time you decide to give him a bath.

But, at least now he smells a lot better.

To bathe a cat takes brute force, perseverance, courage of conviction and a cat. The last ingredient is usually hardest to come by.

— Stephen Baker

I don't think it is so much the actual bath that most cats dislike; I think it's the fact that they have to spend a good part of the day putting their hair back in place.

— Debbie Peterson

One is never sure, watching two cats washing each other, whether it's affection, the taste, or a trial run for the jugular.

— Helen Thomson

WHO OWNS WHO?

"I once had a cat, or should I say, she once had me." So sang John Lennon. In a parallel universe.

Do you own a cat?

Honestly?

Does your cat cater to your every need? Scratch your neck and rub your belly? Buy you playthings? Keep photos of you on its phone? Talk with other cats about you? Keep a cabinet full of human supplies on hand? Does your cat even have a *name* for you?

As every cat owner knows, nobody owns a cat.

— Ellen Perry Berkeley

People don't choose or own cats. Cats choose the people they want to own.

— Warren Eckstein

Cats are kindly masters, just so long as you remember your place.

— Paul Gray

Cats have a scam going — you buy the food, they eat the food, they go away. That's the deal.

— Eddie Izzard

A cat isn't fussy — just so long as you remember he likes his milk in the shallow, rose-patterned saucer and his fish on the blue plate. From which he will take it, and eat it off the floor.

— Arthur Bridges

On training cats

I had been told that the training procedure with cats was difficult. It's not. Mine had me trained in two days.

— Bill Dana

The phrase "domestic cat" is an oxymoron.

— George Will

It is perhaps easier for a cat to train a man than for a man to train a cat. A cat who desires to live with human beings makes it his business to see that the so-called superior race behaves in the proper manner toward him.

— Carl Van Vechten

There are many intelligent species in the universe. They are all owned by cats.

— Unknown

The Ten Catmandments

1. I am the Lord of thy house.

2. Thou shalt have no other pets before me.

3. Thou shalt not ever ignore me.

4. I shall ignore thou when I feel like it.

5. Thou shalt be grateful that I even give thee the time of day.

6. Remember my food dish and keep it full.

7. Thou shalt spend most of thy money on toys and gifts for me.

8. Thou shalt always have thy lap ready for me to curl up in.

9. Thou shalt shower me with love and attention upon demand.

10. Above all, thou shalt do anything and everything it takes to keep me happy.

— Unknown

People who belong to Siamese cats must make up their minds to do a good deal of waiting upon them.

— Sir Compton Mackenzie

The cat is the only animal which accepts the comforts but rejects the bondage of domesticity.

— Georges Louis Leclerc de Buffon

Your cat does not caress you, it caresses itself against you.

— Stendhal (Henri Beyle)

The cat who doesn't act finicky soon loses control of his owner.

— Morris the Cat

Does your cat own you?

Food & meals

- At the store, do you pick up the cat food and kitty litter before you pick out anything for yourself?

- Do you microwave your cat's food? Prepare it from scratch?

- Do you feed your cat tidbits from the table with your fork?

- Does your cat sit at the table (or *on* the table) when you eat?

- Do you have more than four opened but rejected cans of cat food in the refrigerator?

- Does your cat eat out of cut crystal stemware because you both watched the same commercial on television?

Beds & sleep

- Do you sleep in the same position all night because it annoys your cats when you move?

- Does your cat sleep on your head? Do you like it?

- Do you climb out of bed over the headboard or footboard, so you won't disturb the sleeping cat?

- Do you put off making the bed until the cat gets up?

Friends & relationships

- When someone new comes to your house, do you introduce your cat by name to them?

- When people call to talk to you on the phone, do you insist that they say a few words to your cat as well?

- Do you select your friends based on how well your cats like them?

- Would you rather spend a night at home with your cat than go out on a bad date?

- Do you accept dates only with those who have a cat? If so, do you eventually double-date with the cats to see how they get along?

Sundays & holidays

- Does your cat "insist" on a fancy Sunday breakfast consisting of an omelet made from eggs, milk, and salmon, halibut, or trout?

- Do you cook a special turkey for your cat on holidays?

- Do you give your cat presents and a stocking at Christmas? Do you spend more for your cat than you do for your spouse?

- Do the Christmas cards you send out feature your cat sitting on Santa's lap? Does your cat sign the card?

Litter & the litterbox

- Do you buy more than 50 pounds of cat litter a month?

- Do you scoop out the litter box after each use? Do you wait at the box with the scoop in your hand?

Habits & behaviors

- Do you have pictures of your cat in your wallet? Do you bring them out when your friends share pictures of their children? (Pollsters claim 40% of cat owners carry their pet's pictures in their wallets.)

- Does your desire to collect cats intensify during times of stress?

- Will you stand at the open door indefinitely in the freezing rain while your cat sniffs the door, deciding whether to go out or stay in?

- Do you think it's cute when your cat swings on the drapes or licks the butter?

- Do you admit to non-cat owners how many cats you really have?

- Do you watch bad TV because the cat is sleeping on the remote?

- Did you buy a videotape of fish swimming in an aquarium to entertain your cat?

- Do you kiss your cat on the lips?

— Unknown

A cat allows you to sleep on the bed. On the edge.

— Jenny De Vries

Garfield's Law: Cats instinctively know the precise moment their owners will awaken . . . then they awaken them ten minutes sooner.

— Jim Davis

A cat is there when you call her — if she doesn't have something better to do.

— Bill Adler

ADVICE FROM CATS

If cats could talk . . . it might pay you to listen.

Trust the Person Who Feeds You Regularly

Some people lie. Some people disappoint. And some people are so dumb they make the Three Stooges look like the architects of the Manhattan Project by comparison. But anyone who wakes up every day to make sure you are properly fed is the very person you can trust with all your heart.

Unless they go to the bathroom first. Or make their own breakfast first. Or suddenly switch food brands on you. Or try to hide a pill in your breakfast. Or place your water too close to your food. Or don't let you eat someone else's food when you're done with yours. Then it's like you're all alone in this world.

What's Theirs Is Now Yours

Relationships are about two loving individuals coming together to cram all their things into one tiny studio apartment. That's why it makes perfect sense to assume your partner's belongings are now yours, no matter how well or how high they hide them. After all, the word "share" is jumbled right into the word "relationship." (So is the word "purloin" if you misspell it.)

So run off with their favorite socks. Reach into their beverage for one of their ice cubes, olives, or just to see what 21-year-old Scotch feels like. Play with their every possession, even the ones described as "fine china." The more you treat it all as communal property, the more you don't have to worry about breaking a few things.

Show Appreciation So Your Partner Keeps Giving You Stuff

There is a word we cats have when we want to say "Thank you" but we all forgot what it is. Still, it's important to show some nod of appreciation when your partner does something special for you, like get you a toy. Or, even better, two toys (even if one of them is actually an inhaler they bought for themselves). Otherwise, your person will stop getting you anything at all, leaving you with nothing to do but desperately convince yourself that the game "Bat Around the Recently Discarded Bandage" has all the continental elegance of high-stakes baccarat.

Take a Trip Together by Leaving First

Do you spend too many of your weekends snuggled up on the couch with your loved one? Take a holiday from the usual by suddenly departing unnoticed. After a few hours your partner will realize you're missing and commence a frantic search. And that's when an exciting trip begins as they explore sights they rarely ever visit — like crawl spaces and underneath patios — looking for you.

Return just as suddenly by nightfall or the following morning and listen as they recount tales of wandering wild-eyed on all fours trying to find you. Then smile warmly, relishing the great memories you made together.

— All of the above from Francesco Marciuliano, *You Need More Sleep: Advice from Cats*

THE FUR AND THE PURR

When you think of cats, what sounds do you think of?

The meow and the purr. Of course. Cats also trill, growl, chatter, hiss, beep, burble, and wail. But these sounds aren't a big part of their brand.

How do cats purr? Scientists are still not totally sure. The feline family has kept that a closely guarded secret for 25 million years.

Did you know that cats that roar (lions and tigers) cannot purr? And cats that can purr cannot roar? We didn't think so.

Did you know that other animals besides cats can purr? Humans, of course. No, wait — that's *snoring*.

But civets, mongoose, bears, badgers, foxes, hyenas, rabbits, squirrels, guinea pigs, tapirs, ring-tailed lemurs, and gorillas — they can all purr. What could be more satisfying than stroking the belly of a purring hyena or tapir stretched across your lap?

Stroking a purring *cat*, that's what. That's the cat's jammies.

Their power is worthy of awe
These creatures of cuspidate claw
    A mere stroke of their fur —
    They respond with a purr —
You're a pawn in the palm of their paw

— Robert Wilde

Cats are a waste of fur.

— Rita Rudner

If purring could be encapsulated, it'd be the most powerful anti-depressant on the pharmaceutical market.

— Alexis F. Hope

The cat is a dilettante in fur.

— Theophile Gautier

from The Onion

NEWS IN BRIEF

Frustrated Man Doesn't Know What Else He Can Do To Get Cat Purring

EAU CLAIRE, WI — Growing increasingly exasperated by the animal's indifference to his attempts at affection, local man Joe Dooney told reporters Friday that he didn't know what else he could do to get his cat, Harvey, purring. "I tried scratching at his ears, gently stroking his tail, and rubbing the fur on his belly, but he's giving me nothing," said Dooney, adding that nuzzling the 3-year-old cat's face and whispering "you're my special little guy" also proved to be ineffective. "I put him on my lap and used both hands to scratch under his chin and pet his back at the same time, but all he did was lick my arm and go back to sitting there. Christ, I can't get a goddamn peep out of him." At press time, sources confirmed that the ungrateful little bastard had run off.

Purring is an automatic safety-valve device for dealing with an excess of happiness.

— Unknown

No amount of time can erase the memory of a good cat, and no amount of masking tape can ever totally remove his fur from your couch.

— Leo Dworken

To err is human, to purr is feline.

— Robert Byrne

I purr, therefore I am.

— Unknown

FAKE MEWS

Cats often look at you like they're on the verge of saying something. But then they never do. Cat got their tongue, apparently.

If cats could talk, they wouldn't.

— Nan Porter

If cats could talk, they would lie to you.

— Rob Kopack

If a cat spoke, it would say things like, "Hey, I don't see the problem here."

— Roy Blount, Jr.

When a cat speaks, it's because it has something to say, unlike humans who are the great refuse containers of speech.

— V.L. Allineare

My cat does not talk as respectfully to me as I do to her.

— Colette

A cat's got her own opinion of human beings. She don't say much, but you can tell enough to make you anxious not to hear the whole of it.

— Jerome K. Jerome, *Idle Thoughts of an Idle Fellow* (1890)

I've been trying to train my cat to understand the meaning of the word "no." Which seems to be roughly equivalent to teaching a dog Latin.

— Judy Brown

A cat's top ten thoughts

- I could have sworn I heard a can opener.

- Is there something I'm not getting when humans make noise with their mouths?

- Why doesn't the government do something about dogs?

- I wonder if Morris really liked 9-lives, or did he have ulterior motives?

- Hmm . . . If dogs serve humans, and humans serve cats, why can't we ever get those stupid dogs to do anything for us?

- This looks like a good spot for a nap.

- Hey – no kidding, I'm sure that's the can opener.

- Would humans have built a vast and complex civilization of their own if we cats hadn't given them a reason to invent sofas and can openers in the first place?

- If there's a God, how can He allow neutering?

- If that really was the can opener, I'll play finicky just to let them know who's boss!

A guide to understanding your cat

ACTION AND MEANING

- Staring at the food dish = Feed me

- Staring at the cupboard = Feed me

- Licking the empty bowl = Feed me

- Looking at you, taking two steps, looking at you again = Follow me to the kitchen and feed me

- Looking at your lap = Okay, you seem to like it when I sit on you — then will you feed me?

- Sitting on your head = Wake up and feed me

- Scratching at the bedroom door = Wake up, open this door and FEED ME.

- Meow, Meow, Meowrrr = Feed me, feed me, feed me NOW!

- Burp = Thank you!

Katzengrammar

Cats are the type of animal that, if they could, they would correct your grammar.

— Unknown

You may say a cat uses good grammar. Well, a cat does — but you let a cat get excited once; you let a cat get to pulling fur with another cat on a shed, nights, and you'll hear grammar that will give you the lockjaw. Ignorant people think it's the noise which fighting cats make that is so aggravating, but it ain't so; it is the sickening grammar they use.

— Mark Twain

Last year a team of scientists published the results of an extensive study of cat language. They determined that although cats may demonstrate a wide variety of vocalizations, they actually only have two phrases that are translatable into human terms: 1. Hurry up with that food. 2. Everything here is mine.

— Unknown

The Cat's Dictionary

Alcatraz — A penitentiary facility named after the infamous cat burglar Al "Cat" Raz, who, after decades of eluding capture, was finally apprehended and imprisoned there, his name becoming synonymous with the place. Whether intentionally or not, Alcatraz became home to many other notorious criminals named Al — Al Capone, Al Jolson, Al Pacino, Al Green, Al Gore, Al Franken.

cataclysm — a large-scale and violent event involving a cat or cats. For examples, see below.

catalyze — Earlier form of "cat-lies," i.e., the stories cats tell their owners in denying responsibility for such cataclysms as shredding the couch or other furniture.

catalyst — Earlier form of "catalist," or "cat-list," i.e., an enumeration of items one needs to get or do for one's cat.

catalonia — An expression commonly heard from one's friends when asking their opinion on whether one should get a cat, indicating that a cat will take over your life.

catamaran — The southern drawl pronunciation of "cat-a-moron," or "cat-moron," i.e., a stupid cat.

catarrh — The excessive buildup or discharge of cats in the nose, throat, or home, associated with inflammation of mucous membranes or emotions.

Catar — A small, exotic Arabian country on the Persian Gulf, whose chief distinction is that it is ruled by cats (a form of government known as "catocracy").

catastrophe — An obscure punctuation mark related to the apostrophe. Whereas the apostrophe (originally, "apawstrophe") is formed with a single claw mark (e.g., cat's got my tongue), the catastrophe is formed with all five claws on the forepaw — the cat""""s pajamas, the cat""""s meow.

catatonic — Relating to catatonia, the state of immobility and stupor cats enter during extended catnaps.

catenation — Alternate form of "cat-nation," a country where cats either rule or are prized.

caterpillar — A non-load-bearing pillar covered with carpet or other similar surface, intended for cats to use for scratching so that they do not scratch and damage furniture or other household objects.

caterwaller — Similar to the caterpillar (above): a part of a wall intended for cats to scratch. Not to be confused with "caterwauler," to make a yowling noise, as a cat in heat.

catnap — A short, light sleep such as a cat takes.

catnape — The back of a cat's neck, a preferred area for scratching.

catnip — A perennial, herbaceous plant known for the intense attraction its leaves hold for cats. Also "catmint."

catnope — The response cats communicate when you endeavor to have them do something they do not wish to do, such as taking a bath, climbing down from a tree, coming when summoned, or replying when you speak to them.

catnup — Shortened form of "cat nuptial," or a cat wedding. Related to "cat-prenup," a prenuptial agreement between cats.

catsup — Expression commonly used by cat owners when awakened early in the morning by caterwauling or some other such noise from their cat or cats.

concatenate — To link cats together in a chain or series.

escatology — A branch of theology concerned with the final events of history or ultimate destiny of humanity, specifically the doctrine that at the end of days, cats will rule the world.

scat — The word people used to say to their cats to induce them to relocate. Cats, of course, rarely responded, even when the word was shouted. Cat owners consequently developed a wide variety of other sounds aimed at accomplishing this goal — bizarre syllables intended to disconcert and destabilize the cat so as to incite motion. Typical sounds included "doo-be-doo-be-doo," "shoo-doo-shoo-bee-ooo-bee," "louie-ooie-la-la-la," "dot da-ba dot da doo-ba," "ba da 'n' da-ba doo-dot," "doot-n doodle-n dot-n dweedle-ee du-ee-ah." Cat owners who were also jazz singers — Jelly Roll Morton, Ella Fitzgerald, many others — began to incorporate these sounds into their performances when songs were extended and they had run out of lyrics. Unlike cats, however, human audiences were mesmerized. The sounds had the effect of hypnotic, shamanistic incantations. Some observers suggested the singers were sending subliminal messages to their listeners. This manner of singing evolved into rap and hip-hop. To this day, however, cats do not attend these performances.

Saskatchewan — An extension of the term "saskat," or "sass-cat," meaning "sassy cat," i.e., a cat that brazenly exhibits behaviors it knows its owners dislike. Saskatchewan, a fusion of the words "sass-cat" and "chew-on," refers to any object the sassy cat masticates in defiance of its owner, e.g., the owner's couch, shoes, ankles, ears, or other body parts, particularly when the owner is sleeping.

— Robert Wilde

CATS & WOMEN

Women and cats will do as they please, and men and dogs should relax and get used to the idea.

— Robert A. Heinlein

The way to a woman's heart is through her cat

So you're dating a gal who shares her residence with a cat. If your relationship is going to get anywhere, I encourage you to follow each of these suggestions:

- Never, ever mention that you can (or can't) smell the litter box.

- If the kitten wants to spend an hour untying your shoelace, let him. When he gets it untied, retie it so he can continue playing.

- Never make a big show of brushing the cat fur from your slacks.

- Get in the habit of putting a couple of sardines in your pocket — slip them to the cat when she isn't watching. (Note: You may have to do this through the entire dating period, because the cat will likely go for your pocket each time you visit.)

- Don't push the cat off the sofa if he's inserted himself between the two of you.

- If he's still sitting between the two of you when you get amorous, reassure him (mental telepathy is fine) that you have no harmful intentions against his companion, and move him gently to your lap. Try to keep one hand stroking the cat at all times in this situation.

- If you're spending the night, do yourself a favor and don't even TRY to sleep in the cat's favorite spot on the bed.

- When you phone her, ask about her cat.

- When she leaves the room to fix cocktails or check on dinner, ask her if she's got a cat toy handy so you can keep the cat entertained.

- If you're taking her out to dinner, ask her if it's okay to bring home a "cat bag" of leftovers for the cat.

— Glenda Moore

from The Onion

NEWS

Vacationing Woman Thinks Cats Miss Her

VERO BEACH, FL–Annette Davrian, a 45-year-old Cedar Rapids, IA, bank teller, is spending her vacation time in a delusional haze this week, somehow managing to convince herself that her cats actually miss her.

"Buttons is so sensitive, I just know she's scared and frightened without her Mommy by her side," Davrian told uninterested relatives Monday, just hours after arriving in Florida. "And Bonkers gets so cranky when he doesn't get his morning treats. I hope they'll be able to handle this emotionally. I've always gone to great lengths to assure them that they're loved, but they've never been left alone this long before. If they think I've abandoned them, I'd never be able to forgive myself."

Animal behaviorists agree that cats are incapable of feeling sadness over an owner's absence, asserting that their only reaction to such an event would be a brief adjustment period to claim household territory previously thought to be the owner's.

Davrian, who has lived alone since the death of her mother nine years ago, has considered cutting her vacation short because of the cats' nonexistent longing for her to return.

"Those poor, precious kitties," she told a man in an elevator. "I'm all they've got in this world. What will they do without me?"

According to coworker Phil Gross, Davrian began worrying about her cats' imaginary sadness over her Florida trip nearly three weeks before leaving. On Jan. 8, Davrian expressed concern to Gross that the cats might not sufficiently "bond" with a stranger entrusted with their care. Based on this worry alone, she delayed her trip for two weeks, paying a large rescheduling fee for her plane ticket.

"She asked me to look after the cats while she was gone," neighbor Janet Pullman said. "I said sure, figuring I'd just have to feed them. Turns out, she wanted me to go in there three times a day and stay at least 20 minutes each time so the cats would feel 'adequately socialized.' Then she hands me a list of things to do that's, like, 40 items long."

Pullman admitted that she has not followed the elaborate instructions, merely filling up the cats' food and water bowls when they are empty.

"I just dump some Purina in the bowl, and I'm gone," Pullman said. "And do the cats give a shit? No, they do not. Why? Because they're cats."

Hoping to ease the pain and loneliness of her asocial, predatory pets, Davrian has left numerous long messages on her answering machine, claiming that the cats will appreciate hearing her voice. She also wrapped one of her sweaters around a pillow before leaving so Buttons and Bonkers would 'have a bit of me to snuggle with,' unaware that the cats' motivation for 'snuggling' is to maintain body temperature, not to feel emotionally connected to their food provider.

As a supplement to the answering-machine messages, Davrian left the clock radio playing in the bathroom "to keep the little ones company." Though the cats could not care less about the radio, the same cannot be said of neighbor Bob Franz, 49, whose bathroom shares a heating vent with Davrian's.

"I once heard [Davrian] say that [Bonkers] will get lonely without a human voice around to make him feel reassured," Franz said. "But the thing just sits in the window and watches birds all day, just the way it did before she left, and just the way it'll keep on doing after she gets back, every day until one of the two of them dies. Meantime, the damn radio yabbers on all day and night. That radio's probably more aware that the woman's gone than Bonkers."

The Florida excursion is not the first time Davrian has ruined her leisure time fretting about the cats. Since 1996, she has failed to enjoy 219 activities or excursions, including two trips to Lake Winnepesaukee, a visit to a local botanical garden, 23 movies, and three dinners—each of which she spent worrying about being "out of phone contact in case something goes wrong."

Davrian could not be reached for additional comment, as she had just cut short a sailing trip in order to, as brother-in-law Don Koechley said, "make sure the damn cats are okay."

Why do women love cats?

I've never understood why women love cats. Cats are independent, they don't listen, they don't come in when you call, they like to stay out all night, come home and expect to be fed and stroked, then want to be left alone and sleep. In other words, every quality that women hate in a man, they love in a cat.

— Unknown

CATS & KIDS

They may have different-sized brains, cats and kids. And kids grow larger than cats eventually — but the joys and frustrations can be pretty similar sometimes.

Cats are better than kids because they . . .

- Eat less

- Don't ask "Why?"

- Love naps

- Don't lie

- Don't ask for money

- Don't need potty training

- Can entertain themselves without video games and cellphones

- Will never drive your car

- Don't hang out with druggy friends

- Don't smoke or drink

- Don't want the latest fashions, or any fashions

- Can take of themselves unsupervised

- Don't need $150,000 for college

- If they get pregnant, you give the kittens away

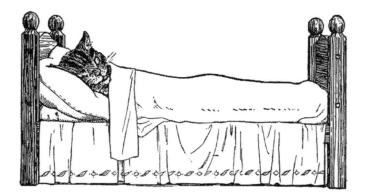

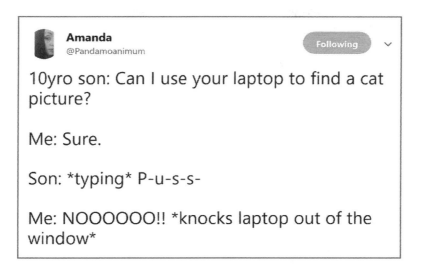

Amanda
@Pandamoanimum

Following ⌄

10yro son: Can I use your laptop to find a cat picture?

Me: Sure.

Son: *typing* P-u-s-s-

Me: NOOOOOO!! *knocks laptop out of the window*

What teenagers have in common with cats

For those of you with teenagers, it may help you to know how much your teens have in common with cats:

- Neither teenagers nor cats turn their heads when you call them by name.

- No matter what you do for them, it's never enough.

- You rarely see a cat walking outside of the house with an adult human. Likewise, no teenager can bear being seen in public with his or her parents.

- Even if you tell jokes as well as Jimmy Fallon, neither your cat nor your teen will ever crack a smile.

- No cat or teenager shares your taste in music.

- Cats and teenagers can lie on the sofa for hours without moving, barely breathing.

- Cats have nine lives. Teenagers act as if they did.

- Cats and teenagers yawn in exactly the same manner — with a sense of complete and utter boredom.

- Cats and teenagers do not improve anyone's furniture.

- Cats free to roam outside are apt to deposit a dead animal in your bedroom. Teenagers are not above that sort of behavior.

So if you need advice about your teens, your best sources are not other parents but veterinarians. It's also helpful to keep a cat guidebook handy.

And when you put out the food, remember: Do not make any sudden moves in their direction.

When they make up their minds, they will finally come to you for some affection and comfort, and it will be a triumphant moment for all.

— Unknown

CATS & MEN

Men who have six or more cats are practicing witchcraft.

— Rita Rudner, *Rita Rudner's Guide to Men*

Periwinkle Jones
@peachesanscream

Following

New boyfriend is allergic to kitten so can't keep him :(He's ginger & named Tom. Friendly. Comes when called. 28yrs-old & works in IT.

I got rid of my husband. The cat was allergic.

— Unknown

A man is like a cat; chase him and he will run — sit still and ignore him and he'll come purring at your feet.

— Helen Rowland

My husband said it was him or the cat. . . . I miss him sometimes.

— Unknown

CATS & PEOPLE

A dog is a dog, a bird is a bird, and a cat is a person.

— Mugsy Peabody

As soon as they're out of your sight, you are out of their mind.

— Walter de la Mare

 beth, an alien
@bourgeoisalien

My cat and I pass each other in the hall without even making eye contact. I think we both know we're just living a lie now.

Cats have brushed against my ankle on crossing my way for so long that my gait, both at home and out of doors, has been compared to that of a man wading through low surf.

— Roy Blount, Jr.

from The Onion

NEWS IN BRIEF

Study: 90% Of All Meowing Comes From Owners Trying To Get Cats To Meow Back

LEWISBURG, PA—Refuting one of the most fundamental assumptions about feline behavior, a new study published Wednesday by researchers at Bucknell University found that 90 percent of all meowing actually comes from owners trying to get their cats to meow back. "We observed that meowing was exceedingly rare among common housecats and that nine out of 10 of such vocalizations came from the animal's owner kneeling down at eye level and repeating the word 'meow' in an effort to get the cat to respond in kind," said lead researcher Gwynne LaRochelle, adding that while only 6 percent of cats meowed back, 20 percent jabbed a paw at its owner's head, 37 percent got up and walked away, and the remainder simply sat impassively as if the meowing had not even occurred. "In fact, the marked discrepancy in the number of meows emitted by the two species raises the rather profound question of whether a meow is actually more of a human sound than a cat sound in the first place." LaRochelle went on to say related research confirmed that 90 percent of barking came from dogs themselves and continued for several uninterrupted minutes once it started.

When my cats aren't happy, I'm not happy. Not because I care about their mood but because I know they're just sitting there thinking up ways to get even.

— Penny Ward Moser

In my more depressed moments, I believe my cats suffer from Stockholm syndrome. You know, where the hostage falls in love with the captor, as an adaptive mechanism.

— Betsy Salkind

I just had a CAT scan. They found cats.

— Paula Poundstone

I'm Catholic. My mother and I were unpacking and she found my diaphragm. I had to tell her it was a bathing cap for my cat.

— Lizz Winstead

People do crazy things when bored. I'm sitting at home with nothing to do, looking at the cats, and think, "I'll teach the cats to wrestle." You should never teach cats to wrestle, but if you do, here's how: Get two cats. Take cat number one, and rub catnip all over him. Put him next to cat number two. The rest just sort of happens.

— Basil White

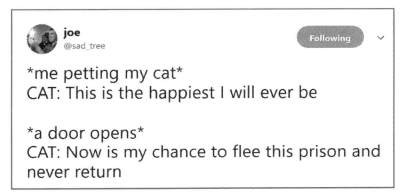

My cat was up all night throwing up. So obviously I was up all night holding her hair.

— Sarah Silverman

A black cat crossing your path signifies that the animal is going somewhere.

— Groucho Marx

When a cat shuts its eyes, you disappear.

— Leonard Michaels

from Jerome K. Jerome

Another cat I had used to get drunk regularly every day. She would hang about for hours outside the cellar door for the purpose of sneaking in on the first opportunity, and lapping up the drippings from the beer cask. I do not mention this habit of hers in praise of the species, but merely to show how almost human some of them are. If the transmigration of souls is a fact, this animal was certainly qualifying most rapidly for a Christian, for her vanity was only second to her love of drink.

— *The Idle Thoughts of an Idle Fellow* (1890)

After scolding one's cat one looks into its face and is seized by the ugly suspicion that it understood every word. And has filed it for reference.

— Charlotte Gray

from The Onion

NEWS IN BRIEF

Dignified Cat Dressed In Adorable, Painful Sweater

DENVER — In an act entirely unbefitting his refined and dignified stature, stately local cat Smokey was placed in an adorable, painful sweater Thursday, multiple sources confirmed. "Aw, look at you — you're so precious," said Smokey's owner, Francine Heatherton, who reportedly spent several minutes forcing the cute and severely constricting article of clothing over the self-respecting feline's forelimbs and torso. "I bet you just feel so warm and cuddly in your sweet little [profoundly uncomfortable and itchy] sweater." At press time, Heatherton debased the otherwise noble and distinguished animal even further by posting a charming, utterly humiliating photo of the sweater-clad cat to her Facebook page.

The cat is domestic only as far as suits its own ends.

— Hector Hugh Munro

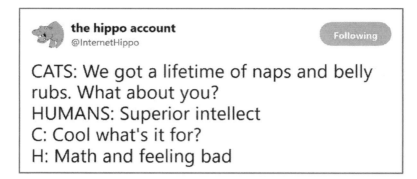

from Dave Barry

People often become deranged by pets. Derangement is the only possible explanation for owning a cat, an animal whose preferred mode of communication is to sink its claws three-quarters of an inch into your flesh. Heaven help the cat-owner who runs out of food. It's not uncommon to see an elderly woman sprinting through the supermarket with one or more cats clinging, leechlike, to her leg as she tries desperately to reach the pet-food section before collapsing from blood loss.

— *Dave Barry Talks Back*

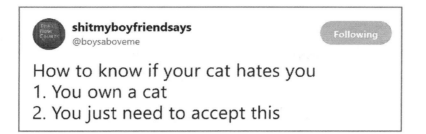

I don't get no respect. When I played in the sandbox, the cat kept covering me up.

— Rodney Dangerfield

I have noticed that what cats most appreciate in a human being is not the ability to produce food, which they take for granted — but his or her entertainment value.

— Geoffrey Household

If you yell at a cat, you're the one who is making a fool of himself.

— Unknown

from Ellen DeGeneres

Though I have dogs now, for most of my life I've had cats as pets. I, personally (in some ways, but not in others), like cats more than dogs (with no offense meant to either Bootsie or Muffin). But have you ever had a cat in heat? They just change on you. Once she was my kitten, my adorable little pet. Then, she's a hooker. I went into the bathroom one night, and she was putting on mascara. "*To*-night, *to*-night, won't be just any . . . lal a. Hm, hm." She didn't know the whole song. "Hm, hm." She just knew some of the words. "Hm, hm."

She was an indoor cat, but male cats knew she was in there somehow. They were just all around the house and somehow she was sneaking out because one morning I found a stamp on her paw. I wouldn't have noticed, but I had just bought this new black light, and she passed right under it. "Hey! What is that?" I said.

And the male cats, they were sneaky the way they tried to get in to see her. One of them disguised himself as a UPS man. He had the truck, the packages, everything. I said, "I'm not falling for that." The suit was just hanging off of him, his little name tag said "Fluffy." "Oh, right. I will not sign here. Scoot!" He went off all mad in that big truck, stripping the gears. They don't know how to drive! Cats.

He came back the next day as a cable repairman. Same outfit, little butt crack hanging out this time. So he fooled me. I let him in. He got me

Nickelodeon for free, hooked that up somehow. So now I get to see all the old shows.

Smart cat — I'd like to see his test scores!

— *My Point . . . and I Do Have One*

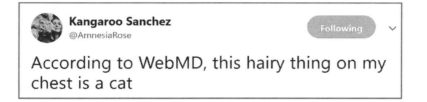

from Dave Barry

But I am not kidding about the Arson Cat. According to an Associated Press story also alertly sent in by numerous readers, investigators concluded that a house fire in Lima, N.Y., was caused by "a cat playing with matches," prompting us to once again ask ourselves, as concerned citizens, when the government is going to come to its senses and order the mandatory sterilization of all cat owners.

— *Dave Barry Talks Back*

from Jerome K. Jerome

As for cats, they nearly equal human beings for vanity. I have known a cat to get up and walk out of the room, on a remark derogatory to her species being made by a visitor, while a neatly turned compliment will set them purring for an hour.

I do like cats. They are so unconsciously amusing. There is such a comic dignity about them, such an "How dare you!" "Go away, don't touch me" sort of air. Now there is nothing haughty about a dog. They are, "Hail, fellow, well met" with every Tom, Dick, or Harry that they come across. When I meet a dog of my acquaintance, I slap his head, call him opprobrious epithets, and roll him over on his back; and there he lies, gaping at me, and doesn't mind it a bit.

Fancy carrying on like that with a cat! Why, she would never speak to you again as long as you lived. No, when you want to win the approbation of a cat you must mind what you are about, and work your way carefully. If you don't know the cat, you had best begin by saying, "Poor pussy." After which, add, "did 'urns," in a tone of soothing sympathy. You don't know what you mean, any more than the cat does, but the sentiment seems to imply a proper spirit on your part, and generally touches her feelings to such an extent that, if you are of good manners and passable appearance, she will stick her back up and rub her nose against you. Matters having reached this stage, you may venture to chuck her under the chin, and tickle the side of her head, and the intelligent creature will then stick her claws into your legs; and all is friendship and affection, as so sweetly expressed in the beautiful lines —

I love little Pussy, her coat is so warm,

And if I don't tease her, she'll do me no harm;

So I'll stroke her, and pat her, and feed her with food,

And Pussy will love me because I am good.

The last two lines of the stanza give us a pretty true insight into pussy's notions of human goodness. It is evident that in her opinion goodness consists of stroking her, and patting her, and feeding her with food. I fear this narrow-minded view of virtue, though, is not confined to pussies. We are all inclined to adopt a similar standard of merit in our estimate of other people.

— *The Idle Thoughts of an Idle Fellow* (1890)

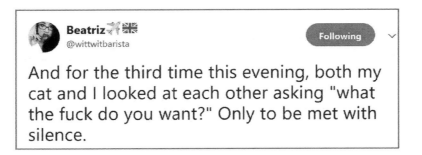

Beatriz ✈️🇬🇧
@wittwitbarista

Following ⌄

And for the third time this evening, both my cat and I looked at each other asking "what the fuck do you want?" Only to be met with silence.

from Dave Barry

I once, as a favor to my sister, transported her cat in my car about ninety miles to her new apartment. Naturally it turned out that the only place in the entire car that the cat wanted to be was directly under the brake pedal, which meant that if I needed to slow down, I had to reach down there and grab the cat without looking — an activity comparable to groping around for a moray eel in a dark underwater cave filled with barbed wire — and then I'd hurl the cat, still clinging to pieces of my flesh, into the backseat, and then I'd hit the brakes, and then the cat would scuttle back under the pedal. As you can imagine, this cat and I were the best of friends by the time we arrived at my sister's apartment, and I only hope that I see it again someday when my hand has healed to the point where I can aim a dart gun.

— *Homes and Other Black Holes*

Curiosity killed the cat. But for a while I was a suspect.

— Steven Wright

Cats regard people as warm-blooded furniture.

— Jacquelyn Mitchard, *The Deep End of the Ocean*

 **Raspberry Jam**
@Jenny4ashley

 Following

None of my friends laugh at any of my jokes because cats can only meow.

The trouble with sharing one's bed with cats is that they'd rather sleep on you than beside you.

— Pam Brown

My cat is depressed. I had the exterminators in and they killed all his toys.
— Anita Wise

That cat will write her autograph all over your leg if you let her.

— Mark Twain

I found out why cats drink out of the toilet. My mother told me it's because it's cold in there. And I'm like, "How did my mother know that?"

— Wendy Liebman

Audrey Porne
@AudreyPorne

Following

If cats could text you back, they wouldn't.

Beware of people who dislike cats.

— Irish proverb

I'm reading *Hints from Heloise,* and she says that if you put an angora sweater in the freezer for an hour, it won't shed for the rest of the day. And I'm thinking, "My cat sheds an awful lot."

— Ellen DeGeneres

There are two means of refuge from the miseries of life: music and cats.

— Albert Schweitzer

You will always be lucky if you know how to make friends with strange cats.

— Colonial American proverb

Roberto Blizzard
@VeganYogaDude

Following ∨

"Be sure to read the manual before assembling your cat"

Cats and consequences

How you behave toward cats here below determines your status in Heaven.

— Robert A. Heinlein

People that hate cats will come back as mice in their next life.

— Faith Resnick

If I die before my cat, I want a few of my ashes put in his food so I can live inside him.

— Drew Barrymore

Cats are better than people

I have studied many philosophers and many cats. The wisdom of cats is infinitely superior.

— Hippolyte Taine

Of all God's creatures there is only one that cannot be made the slave of the lash. That one is the cat. If man could be crossed with a cat it would improve man, but it would deteriorate the cat.

— Mark Twain

With their qualities of cleanliness, discretion, affection, patience, dignity, and courage, how many of us, I ask you, would be capable of becoming cats?

— Fernand Mery

The more people I meet the more I like my cat.

— Countless humans

And it's an "if" . . .

- If you can start the day without caffeine . . .

- If you can be cheerful, ignoring aches and pains . . .

- If you can resist complaining . . .

- If you can eat the same food every day and be grateful for it . . .

- If you can take criticism and blame without resentment . . .

- If you can face the world without lies and deceit . . .

- If you can conquer tension without medical help . . .

- If you can relax without liquor . . .

- If you can sleep without the aid of drugs . . .

- Then . . . you may be a cat.

— Unknown

CATS IN THE HOUSE

I have a cat at home. She's an indoor cat. She's never been outside. She has no idea that there's even an outdoors. She thinks that when I leave for the day, I'm just standing on the other side of the door for twelve hours.

— Tig Notaro

My cats have fleas, which makes me feel bad because I live in a one-bedroom apartment, and they never go out. So if they got fleas, they got them from me. I feel like an ass for making them wear the collars.

— Paula Poundstone

There's no need for a piece of sculpture in a home that has a cat.

— Wesley Bates

Cat Diary

Day 983 of my captivity

My captors continue to taunt me with bizarre little dangling objects. They dine lavishly on fresh meat, while the other inmates and I are fed hash or some sort of dry nuggets. Although I make my contempt for the rations perfectly clear, I nevertheless must eat something in order to keep up my strength.

The only thing that keeps me going is my dream of escape.

In an attempt to disgust them, I once again vomited on the carpet. Today I decapitated a mouse and dropped its headless body at their feet. I had hoped this would strike fear into their hearts, since it clearly demonstrates what I am capable of. However, they merely made condescending comments about what a "good little hunter" I am.

There was some sort of assembly of their accomplices tonight. I was placed in solitary confinement for the duration of the event. However, I could hear the noises and smell the food. I overheard that my confinement was due to the power of "allergies." I must learn what this means and how to use it to my advantage.

Today I was almost successful in an attempt to assassinate one of my captors by weaving around his feet as he was walking. I must try this tomorrow — but at the top of the stairs.

I am convinced that the other prisoners here are flunkies and snitches. The dog receives special privileges. He is routinely released and seems more than willing to return.

The bird has got to be an informant. I observe him communicating with the guards regularly. I am certain that he reports my every move. My captors have arranged protective custody for him in an elevated cell, so he is safe. For now.

— Unknown

Cats can work out mathematically the exact place to sit that will cause the most inconvenience.

— Pam Brown

It's really the cat's house. I just pay the mortgage.

— Unknown

from The New Yorker

Where I Live

Amy Ozols

Welcome to my apartment. Can I take your coat? Please make yourself at home.

This is my cat.

It's a studio apartment, so there's not much to see, but let me give you a quick tour anyway. Here's the kitchen. It's not very big, but there's a ton of cabinet space, which is nice. Here's my desk, where I do most of my writing, and that's the bathroom over there.

Here is another cat.

This is a picture of my family from last Thanksgiving. Here's my mom — she's a real pistol. I think that's where I get my sense of humor. These are my sisters. My dad's the tall guy in the back. And that's my grandmother, with a cat on her lap. And that animal crouched menacingly on top of the picture frame — that's an actual cat, far more knowledgeable and terrifying than the cat in the picture.

This is my couch, where we can sit and watch a movie later, and then maybe make out awkwardly while three to six cats stare at us.

This cat over here — the one burrowing into your overcoat — belongs to my neighbor. But he comes over a lot, so I feed him and buy him toys and take him to the vet and stuff like that. He's a pretty great cat, so I sort of just let him live here and systematically destroy my clothing and furniture.

This is an antique gramophone I inherited from my grandmother. It's worth a lot of money, but I'm never going to sell it, on account of how much it means to my family.

I'm kidding, of course. It's not really an antique. Or a gramophone. It's a cat.

Do you want a drink? I think I have some beer, or there's a pitcher of water in the fridge. It's tap water, but it's filtered through one of those Brita things, so it tastes pretty good. I also have some bottled water, which I save for the cats, but you're totally welcome to one of the bottled waters, if you want to be a dick about it.

You can probably tell that I'm more of a cat person than a dog person. I'm more of an "all animals" person, actually. I like animals way better than people, because they're friendly and they don't eat very much, and they don't tend to fuck twenty-six-year-old flight attendants under adulterous circumstances, the way humans do.

Are you allergic? There's some stuff coming out of your nose. Don't be embarrassed; it happens to me all the time. In fact, if I'm being totally honest here — and, let's face it, I'm being totally honest here, perhaps unsettlingly so — I haven't breathed freely since the Clinton Administration. But it's a small price to pay, considering how much joy these cats bring into my life. These watchful, almost eerily numerous cats.

I'm sorry about the smell — that's sort of a litter-box issue. It's tough to have eight cats in a studio apartment, but I think while you're spending the night here — the first of many, many passion-filled nights you'll undoubtedly wish to spend here — you'll find that it's well worth the smell to have the selfless companionship of these seventeen reeking, dander-encrusted animals. I said "eight" before when I meant to say "seventeen." That's the number of cats that I have.

I understand that you need to step out for some Claritin, but I'm really looking forward to your coming back. I think we're going to have a lot of fun, you and I, watching movies and eating popcorn and having workmanlike intercourse on the fold-out sofa — all under the penetrating gaze of the vile feline minions with which I have inexplicably chosen to share my home.

I am begging you: please do not tell them I said that. Should they deem it distasteful, we would have zero chance of survival.

Anyway, I'll see you soon. And thanks again for coming over. It's always such a treat to have guests.

from The Onion

NEWS IN BRIEF

Depressed Cat Just Going Through Motions Of Destroying Couch

MUSKOGEE, OK—Halfheartedly ripping at the fabric from an armrest, depressed local cat Harvey on Monday was reportedly just going the motions of destroying a couch. According to sources, the American shorthair that has been listlessly raking deep claw marks into most of the couch's visible surface has been feeling a bit down recently. Reports confirm that, despite it usually being one of his favorite activities, the hours the cat spent tearing the fluff out of the cushions did nothing whatsoever to lift his spirits. Sources later reported that Harvey could barely even muster the energy to kick kitty litter all over the floor.

CAT RULES

FROM A CAT OWNER TO VISITORS

To pacify you, my dear pets, I have posted the following message on our front door:

To all non-pet owners who visit and like to complain about our pets:

They live here. You don't.

If you don't want their hair on your clothes, stay off the furniture. That's why they call it "fur"niture.

I like my pets a lot better than I like most people.

To you, it's an animal. To me, he/she is an adopted son/daughter who is short, hairy, walks on all fours, and doesn't speak clearly.

— Unknown

FROM A CAT TO CATS

Basic Rules for Cats Who Have a House to Run

Gary Bogue

Back in 1991, my now long-deceased Siamese, Isis, compiled a list of "Basic Rules for Cats Who Have a House to Run."

These provocative rules were amazingly well-received. Feral cats from as far away as Tasmania faxed in requests for copies. . . .

Here they are:

Chairs & Rugs

If you have to throw up, get into a chair quickly. If you cannot manage in time, get onto an Oriental rug. If no Oriental rug, shag is good.

Doors

Do not allow closed doors in any room. To get door opened, stand on hind legs and hammer with forepaws. Once door is opened, it is not necessary to use it. After you have ordered an outside door opened, stand halfway in and out and think about several things.

This is particularly important during very cold weather, rain, snow and mosquito season.

Guests

Quickly determine which guest hates cats the most. Sit on that human's lap. If you can arrange to have Friskies Fish 'n' Glop on your breath, so much the better.

For sitting on laps or rubbing against trousers, select fabric color that contrasts well with fur. For example: white-furred cats go to black wool clothing.

For the guest who claims, "I love kitties," be ready with aloof disdain; apply claws to stockings or use a quick nip on the ankle.

When walking among dishes on the dinner table, be prepared to look surprised and hurt when scolded. The idea is to convey, "But you allow me on the table when company isn't here."

Always accompany guests to the bathroom. It is not necessary to do anything. Just sit and stare.

Work

If one of your humans is sewing or writing and another is idle, stay with the busy one. This is called helping, otherwise known as hampering. Following are the rules for hampering:

1. When supervising cooking, sit just behind the left heel of the cook. You cannot be seen and thereby stand a better chance of being stepped on, then picked up and consoled.

2. For book readers, get in close under the chin, between the human's eyes and the book, unless you can lie across the book itself.

3. For knitting projects, curl up quietly onto the lap of the knitter and pretend to doze. Occasionally reach out and slap the knitting needles sharply. This can cause dropped stitches or split yarn. The knitter may try to distract you with a scrap ball of yarn. Ignore it. Remember, the aim is to hamper work.

Play

It is very important. Get enough sleep in the daytime so you are fresh for playing catch mouse or king-o-the-hill on top of their bed between 2 and 4 a.m.

Training

Begin people-training early. You will then have a smooth-running household.

Humans need to know basic rules. They can be taught if you start early and are consistent.

EVALUATING YOUR CAT

from McSweeney's

Cat Performance Review

Kendra Eash

1. Skill and proficiency in carrying out assignments

Inconsistent. When asked to come sit on the couch or get down off of the kitchen table, Stereo's performance is uneven at best. I've also met resistance when assigning her to wear a homemade snowflake hat for our yearly Christmas card and when asking her to stop backing into me, butthole first.

Additionally, while I know that she is able to do a backflip onto the floor, she consistently refuses to perform on command so that I can create a Vine.

2. Possesses skills and knowledge to perform the job competently

Proficient. Stereo is very cute. She doesn't shy away from attention and will allow occasional petting in a well-received manner. Unfortunately her attitude comes off as if she just doesn't care. For example, if I say "Stereo come here" or rapidly pat the couch to indicate next steps, she fails to follow through on a regular basis. This lack of respect is embarrassing for management and guests.

3. Skill at planning, organizing, and prioritizing workload

Highly Effective. I would categorize Stereo's workload as light. She moves effortlessly between eating, sleeping, and staring blankly at the Boston fern. Her grooming seems to be taking a back seat to eating, and I would like to see her pay as much attention to cleaning the middle of her lower back as she does to the bag of treats we keep beneath the sink.

4. Holds self accountable for assigned responsibilities; sees tasks through to completion in a timely manner

Proficient. Stereo sets high standards for herself, consistently finishing any bowl of food put in front of her (her pace is of some concern, as guests have commented that her consumption levels may border on unhealthy at times.)

With that said, there have been a few embarrassing episodes coming out of the litter box, where performance is stuck in media res. When this occurs, Stereo takes immediate action, dragging the bottom of the problem area on the floor until the transaction has been severed appropriately. On these occasions, management (me) has not minded picking up what she left off because of the effort Stereo put forth.

5. Communicates effectively with supervisor and peers

Inconsistent. Too often, Stereo chooses to vocalize her concerns at inconvenient times in a baffling manner (i.e. yowling). Paired with inconsistent behavior, such as marching back and forth on management's head at night, this communication is far from effective, as management has no fucking clue what she wants.

6. Ability to work cooperatively with supervision or as part of a team

Inconsistent. Her peers, primarily our tuxedoed intern, have expressed questions about Stereo's passion for existence, in some cases trailing her through the home to try and spark collaboration. In these instances, Stereo has reacted defensively, a troubling pattern that ends up affecting everyone's ability to follow the plot lines of *Game of Thrones*.

However, Stereo has also inherited some rather messy situations from the intern. When this occurs, she has used tact and directness to cover them with litter and complete her own work.

7. Adeptness at analyzing facts, problem solving, decision-making, and demonstrating good judgment

Unsatisfactory. Stereo's judgment is questionable on occasion. For example, despite having two carpet-covered poles at her disposal, Stereo has continued to liaison with the side of the couch. While some of this may be chalked up to habit, there is no discernible reason that Stereo should continue to make this poor choice, as it has been clearly stated to her that destroying the furniture is not cost-effective.

While she displays quick reaction times and a surprising amount of physical grace for her bulk when playing with toys on a string, she remains consistently fooled by a simple laser pointer. Although amusing for management, this is a troubling inability to discern between illusion and reality, and a blow to her professionalism.

Overall Comments

While Stereo's presence is quite divisive around the office — some have even gone so far as to note an "allergic" reaction to her presence — her strengths in cuteness and companionship continue to outweigh her weaknesses in communication and collaboration. With more individualized attention from management, I see Stereo going as far as the apartment will allow.

CAT HAIKU
PART 2

The food in my bowl
Is old, and more to the point
Contains no tuna.

So you want to play.
Will I claw at dancing string?
Your ankle's closer.

There's no dignity
In being sick — which is why
I don't tell you where.

Seeking solitude
I am locked in the closet.
For once I need you.

Tiny can, dumped in
Plastic bowl. Presentation,
One star; service: none.

Am I in your way?
You seem to have it backwards:
This pillow is taken.

Your mouth is moving;
Up and down, emitting noise.
I've lost interest.

The dog wags his tail,
Seeking approval. See mine?
Different message.

My brain: walnut-sized.
Yours: largest among primates.
Yet, who leaves for work?

Most problems can be
Ignored. The more difficult
Ones can be slept through.

My affection is
conditional. Don't stand up,
It's your lap I love.

Cats can't steal the breath
Of children. But if my tail's
Pulled again, I'll learn.

I don't mind being
Teased, any more than you mind
A skin graft or two.

So you call this thing
Your "cat carrier." I call
These my "blades of death."

Toy mice, dancing yarn
Meowing sounds. I'm convinced:
You're an idiot.

— Unknown

iGNORANCE oF THE CLAW IS NO EXCUSE

We can only imagine the contentious debates in city halls and state legislatures that gave rise to these important laws. But now the citizens of these cities and states rest easily at night, knowing these safety regulations are in place and their government leaders have made their safety their first priority.

At what time can they resume?

Cats are not allowed to howl after 9:00 p.m.

— Columbus, Georgia

And the turn signals also had better be working properly . . .

Cats may not roam freely unless they are wearing a taillight.

— Sterling, Colorado

We say let them do it . . .

Cats are not permitted to chase dogs up telephone poles.

— International Falls, Minnesota

But unlighted is OK . . .

It is illegal for anyone to give lighted cigars to dogs, cats, and other domesticated animal kept as pets.

— Zion, Illinois

So *that's* why there's so much cat and dog action outside the county courthouse . . .

Cats and dogs are not allowed to mate without a permit.

— Ventura County, California

Birds typically cannot hear just two . . .

All cats venturing outside must wear three bells to warn birds of their approach.

— Creskill, New Jersey

This will magically cancel out the double bad luck?

All black cats must wear bells on Friday the 13th.

— French Lick Springs, Indiana

If you cat owners do acquire a pet bird, it will call the police . . .

If you own a cat, you may not have a pet bird. There's a $25 fine for the offense.

— Reed City, Michigan

Rowdy streets can be tough on cats . . .

A cat may not be out on the street if it is rowdy.

— Mississippi

And the penalty?

It is illegal for cats and dogs to fight each other.

— Barber, North Carolina

They're just aching to do it near that place of worship . . .

It is illegal for cats to mate if they are within 1,500 feet of a pub, tavern, school, or place of worship.

— California

If you can't find your car in the morning, you know who took it and why . . .

It is illegal for cats to mate within city limits.

— Oregon

Please have the decency to do it before you arrive . . .

It is illegal to get a cat drunk while in a public park.

— Tuscaloosa, Alabama

Somehow we've never been able to get the number below a dozen . . .

You may not have more than five cats at one time.

— Topeka, Kansas

Once the cats stop looking, then feel free to bother them . . .

Dogcatchers are prohibited from bothering cats while looking for wayward dogs.

— Alabama

STRAY CAT BLUES

Strict, Unbending Rules For Dealing With Stray Cats

- Stray cats will not be fed.

- Stray cats will not be fed anything except dry cat food.

- Stray cats will not be fed anything except dry cat food moistened with a little milk.

- Stray cats will not be fed anything except dry cat food moistened with warm milk, yummy treats and leftover fish scraps.

- Stray cats will not be encouraged to make this house their permanent residence.

- Stray cats will not be petted, played with or picked up and cuddled unnecessarily.

- Stray cats that are petted, played with, picked up and cuddled will absolutely not be given a name.

- Stray cats with or without a name will not be allowed inside the house at any time.

- Stray cats will not be allowed inside the house except at certain times.

- Stray cats will not be allowed inside the house except on days ending in "y."

- Stray cats allowed inside will not be permitted to jump up on or sharpen their claws on the furniture.

- Stray cats will not be permitted to jump up on, or sharpen claws on, the really good furniture.

- Stray cats will be permitted on all furniture but must sharpen claws on new $114.99 sisal-rope cat-scratching post with three perches.

- Stray cats will answer the call of nature outdoors in the sand.

- Stray cats will answer the call of nature in the three-piece, high-impact plastic tray filled with Fresh 'n' Sweet kitty litter.

- Stray cats will answer the call of nature in the hooded litter pan with a three-panel privacy screen and plenty of headroom.

- Stray cats will sleep outside.

- Stray cats will sleep in the garage.

- Stray cats will sleep in the house.

- Stray cats will sleep in a cardboard box lined with an old blanket.

- Stray cats will sleep in the special Kitty-Komfort-Bed with non-allergenic lamb's wool pillow.

- Stray cats will not be allowed to sleep in our bed.

- Stray cats will not be allowed to sleep in our bed, except at the foot.

- Stray cats will not be allowed to sleep in our bed under the covers.

- Stray cats will not be allowed to sleep in our bed under the covers except at the foot.

- Stray cats will not play on the desk.

- Stray cats will not play on the desk near the computer.

- Stray cats are forbidden to walk on the computer keyboard on the desk when the human is asdfjjhhkl;ljfd.;oier'puyykmm4hbdm9lo9jmdskdm USING IT.

— Unknown

WE'VE LOST THAT LOVIN' FELINE . . .

Looking for your cat?

Places where to look: behind the books in the bookshelf, in any cupboard with a gap too small for any cat to squeeze through, at the top of anything beyond reach, under anything too low for a cat to squeeze under, and inside the piano.

— Roseanne Ambrose-Brown

 Kendra Gaylord
@kendragaylord

How many lost cats walk by the telephone pole with their missing flier on it? Just another reason to teach your cat to read.

from The New Yorker

Attention: Lost Cat

Patricia Marx

Reward if you find my cat, Sally. Sally is eleven, but she has the face of a cat much younger. She is taffy-colored and has no distinguishing features except for the spot on her lung. Sally understands eight commands. Nine, if you count "Drop it! Drop the baby!" Sally loves a good steak but will gladly have whatever you are having. If she seems to have trouble swallowing, call Dr. Sidarsky, at (570) 555-1212. Dr. Sidarsky calls every day to ask if Sally is back. Once, Dr. Sidarsky invited me to a tennis match where a little girl who could not speak English beat the defending champion. If you ask me, Dr. Sidarsky has a crush on me. Before Sally was lost, Dr. Sidarsky nominated me for Pet Owner of the Year. When the judges came to our house, Sally would not come down from the breezeway. I'm not saying that was the reason I lost the title, but it cost me points.

Sally was last seen in Kansas, where she fell out of my car — a 1998 yellow Toyota Corolla, Indiana license plate FJ3-JR57. To tell you the truth, Sally didn't actually fall. My ex-husband was trying to push me and my suitcases out of the car and Sally was in the way. I'd opened the door to throw out a pair of pants and some other garbage of my ex-husband's. I hate a messy car. My ex-husband says he was leaning over to close the door, but I definitely felt a nudge. Sally and the gourmet-cooking cassettes that I had taken out of the library landed all over Route 23 in Kansas. Sally ran toward Nebraska. We were on the ramp toward Missouri. My ex-husband's sister Sugar lives in Nebraska. I don't like Sugar and I know Sugar does not like me. She sent me a bathroom scale as a wedding gift. Normally, I have nothing to do with Sugar, but I called her just in case Sally had turned up there. Sometimes animals have a sixth sense about knowing who your relatives are and how to get in touch. As usual, Sugar was unpleasant. She said I sounded like I had gained weight.

Sally has been missing for more than a year, and I am losing hope. Her mother belonged to my grandfather, and now my grandfather is dead. Sally is my last link to my grandfather. If you find Sally and she is dead, send her back anyway. My parents are dead, but I have their steak knives. Once, I had a locket of my grandmother's. I gave it to my daughter for Christmas, since my daughter was named after my grandmother, who was named after her grandmother, who was named after Sally, but not that Sally. When I lost my daughter in the custody suit, I lost the locket, too. I lost everything. Well, not all of the steak knives. Or the weight — I didn't lose that, either.

In spite of what the judge said, my ex-husband is not fit to care for my daughter, pony or no pony. The only things my ex-husband can cook are Texas Tommies. My ex-husband's girlfriend cannot cook, either, but I have to admit, she knows good food.

If I still had Sally, I think the judge would have let me keep my daughter. Pets are a sign of a loving home life. I know the judge would have been impressed if I had been Pet Owner of the Year. I might have gone into politics if I had been Pet Owner of the Year, maybe alderman. I am not too old to get into politics, and I have a lot of ideas. Let's not forget that after the Russian Revolution they turned the stock exchange into an aquarium. For the people! We could do something like that. If Sally came back, I would take a picture of me holding her and use that on my campaign poster. And if she didn't my slogan could be "Help me help you find my cat!" Even if you don't find Sally, please send cash. It's not the same thing as a cat, but it is a consolation.

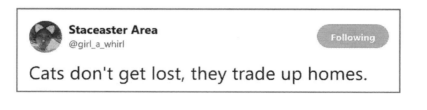

Staceaster Area
@girl_a_whirl

Following

Cats don't get lost, they trade up homes.

CATACLYSMS

One small typo led to a hilarious "cat"astrophic Reddit thread

A Reddit user posed a question to AskReddit about fellow redditors' "worst car accidents." A typo inadvertently entered the thread, and the question became, "What's the worst cat accident you've ever been in?" Here are some replies:

"Caught a stray, got scratched and shat on. My wife handed me a napkin to clean up. She didn't know that the napkin already had mayonnaise on it. I ended up wiping feces and mayo into my open wounds."

"I left cheesecake out one night. My cat got to it, looked like he took a few large bites. Cheesecake didn't sit well with him and he puked, all down my stairs. Probably covered about 6 steps. Took forever to clean and I haven't been able to eat cheesecake since. Cat puke can be the grossest."

"Cat walked over my keyboard while I was doing my taxes. Fortunately I had a receipt showing I donated :SKJD: afds;lka to Goodwill."

"I was taking my cats home for the holidays and 20 minutes into the ride, one of them pooped. It stunk up the whole car and I could barely breathe. I had about an 1.25 hours left in the car, so I decided to gun it. Got pulled over doing 83 MPH in a 65 MPH. Got a fat ticket too :("

"Almost went to the ER because of giving a cat a bath. My roommate's cat got into something nasty, so here we are, 2 full grown dudes struggling to wash this 8-lb kitten. I am in charge of pinning said kitty to the bathtub while my roommate shampoos and cleans the kitty. Kitty's job is to meow in a satanic tone while making constant soul-piercing eye contact with us. In his final fight-or-flight attack to get free, I catch three claws across the inside of my forearm, right across the 2 major veins/arteries. I have a moment of sheer panic, waiting for my arm to explode in a Tarantino-esque blood shower (which would have resulted in another bath for the cat). Thankfully, his claws didn't go very deep and I was spared a trip to the ER and only required some Neosporin and bandaids. It was the cat's first and final bath. Any human cleaning behind that was done with a washcloth by his owner."

"Using a laser pointer with two cats, they had a head on collision. Hope they had inpurrance."

"I woke up and realized I was a 43-year-old woman with 16 cats."

"Stepped on something soft and squishy as I crossed the room to turn the light on. Was a dead mouse."

from The Onion

NEWS IN BRIEF

Study Finds Cats Only Meow When They Want To Alert Owner Of Neighbor's Murder They Witnessed Through Window

LONDON — A new study published this week in the journal *Animal Behaviour* revealed that house cats only meow when they want to alert their owners that they just witnessed a neighbor's murder while looking out a window. "Through direct observation and analysis of feline vocal patterns, we were able to confirm that the sound commonly known as a 'meow' is in fact a signal that a gruesome homicide has just been committed next door," said the study's author and King's College professor Debra T. Shen, Ph.D., noting that if a cat meows during the day, it has seen a shooting or stabbing, whereas a nighttime meow indicates death by strangulation. "It also appears as though the volume and number of meows correlates to the number of victims and the amount of blood — a trait that likely evolved as a way to discreetly call for help without drawing the killer's attention." Shen added that the findings have lent credence to the long-held theory that cats purr to signal that someone is hiding right behind the curtains.

FROM CAT TO VERSE

This poem was written by English poet Christopher Smart (1722–1771), who also wrote articles for popular magazines and was well known around London. This is just the first part of a longer poem called "Jubilate Agno" (you can find the original online). Here's humor from a different world.

For I will consider my cat Jeoffry

For I will consider my Cat Jeoffry.

For he is the servant of the Living God duly and daily serving him.

For at the first glance of the glory of God in the East he worships in his way.

For this is done by wreathing his body seven times round with elegant quickness.

For then he leaps up to catch the musk, which is the blessing of God upon his prayer.

For he rolls upon prank to work it in.

For having done duty and received blessing he begins to consider himself.

For this he performs in ten degrees.

For first he looks upon his forepaws to see if they are clean.

For secondly he kicks up behind to clear away there.

For thirdly he works it upon stretch with the forepaws extended.

For fourthly he sharpens his paws by wood.

For fifthly he washes himself.

For sixthly he rolls upon wash.

For seventhly he fleas himself, that he may not be interrupted upon the
    beat.

For eighthly he rubs himself against a post.

For ninthly he looks up for his instructions.

For tenthly he goes in quest of food.

For having consider'd God and himself he will consider his neighbour.

For if he meets another cat he will kiss her in kindness.

For when he takes his prey he plays with it to give it a chance.

For one mouse in seven escapes by his dallying.

For when his day's work is done his business more properly begins.

For he keeps the Lord's watch in the night against the adversary.

For he counteracts the powers of darkness by his electrical skin and glaring
    eyes.

For he counteracts the Devil, who is death, by brisking about the life.

For in his morning orisons he loves the sun and the sun loves him.

For he is of the tribe of Tiger.

For the Cherub Cat is a term of the Angel Tiger.

Hamlet the Cat

Shakespaw

To go outside, and there perchance to stay

Or to remain within: that is the question:

Whether 'tis better for a cat to suffer

The cuffs and buffets of inclement weather

That Nature rains on those who roam abroad,

Or take a nap upon a scrap of carpet,

And so by dozing melt the solid hours

That clog the clock's bright gears with sullen time

And stall the dinner bell. To sit, to stare

Outdoors, and by a stare to seem to state

A wish to venture forth without delay,

Then when the portal's opened up, to stand

As if transfixed by doubt. To prowl; to sleep;

To choose not knowing when we may once more

Our re-admittance gain: Aye, there's the hairball;

For if a paw were shaped to turn a knob,

Or work a lock or slip a window-catch,

And going out and coming in were made

As simple as the breaking of a bowl,

What cat would bear the household's petty plagues,

The cook's well-practiced kicks, the butler's broom,

The infant's careless pokes, the tickled ears,
The trampled tail, and all the daily shocks
That fur is heir to, when, of his own free will,
He might his exodus or entrance make
With a mere mitten? Who would spaniels fear,
Or strays trespassing from a neighbor's yard,
But that the dread of our unheeded cries
And scratches at a barricaded door
No claw can open up, dispels our nerve
And makes us rather bear our humans' faults
Than run away to unguessed miseries?
Thus caution doth make house cats of us all;
And thus the bristling hair of resolution
Is softened up with the pale brush of thought,
And since our choices hinge on weighty things,
We pause upon the threshold of decision.

The Fool Who Wants a Cat

J. Luke Migliacci

It wasn't very long ago,
Just about a year or so,
When I convinced my husband that
He'd hardly notice one small cat.

He made his position very clear
"She's your responsibility, dear.
This kitten's yours, remember that.
I'm not the fool who wants a cat."

"You'll be in charge of discipline,
Putting her out and letting her in."
Well I understood she'd be my cat,
But I don't think he remembers that.

She's mine to care for and to feed;
I see to her every need.
But when it's time for love and a pat,
She immediately becomes his cat.

He loves "my cat" and it's plain to see
That she loves him as much as me.
At any designated time
You'll find her in his lap not mine.

I suppose I could remind him that
He's not the fool who wants a cat.
But in fact it pleases me,
Because love is better shared by three.

A CAT'S RESUMÉ

ERNIE

Alley #3, Corner Market & Broadway
Los Angeles, CA 10001

Objective

Seeking a long-term position as housecat.

Qualifications

- Omnivorous. Strong rodent-control capabilities.

- Excellent nonverbal communication skills. Highly-developed purring mechanism.

- Affectionate. Adaptable. Rare feline willingness to follow established guidelines.

- Proven stud potential.

Work Experience

BARNCAT — Westchester Estates, New York. December 2016–present.

- Ensured day-to-day rodent and small animal control for two-story, 35,000-square-foot barn.

- Consumed over five rodents per day (average).

- Achieved 37% reduction in barn swallow population.

- Awarded feline leukemia inoculation after one month of service.

- Earned in-house privileges for outstanding service and behavior after only two months on the job.

ALLEYCAT — Wilshire Boulevard, Los Angeles, California. March 2014–November 2016.

- Successfully maintained territorial boundaries of a four-block area in highly competitive and dangerous location.

- Maintained 100% safety record while expertly maneuvering safely and deftly though heavy skateboard, rollerblade, and automobile traffic.

- Developed proficiency in urban survival, hunting, and scavenging skills. Known sire of 77 litters in a nine-month period.

Education

Certificate: Feline Deportment, February 2014.

- Tom & Jerry, Associates, Hollywood, California. 1-year intensive study with Tom of famed "Tom & Jerry" partnership. High honors.

References available on request.

— Unknown

LAWS OF PHYSICS APPLIED TO CATS

Physicists still haven't figured out how cats always land on their feet when they fall — though they claim they're close.

But Japanese scientists have discovered that cats understand basic laws of physics. In fact, the American physicist Jack Hetherington published an influential paper that listed his cat Chester as the coauthor.

Here, from the parallel universe of cats, are the basic laws of cat physics.

- *Law of Cat Inertia* — A cat at rest will tend to remain at rest, unless acted upon by some outside force, such as the opening of cat food, or a nearby scurrying mouse.

- *Law of Cat Motion* — A cat will move in a straight line, unless there is a really good reason to change direction.

- *Law of Cat Magnetism* — All blue blazers and black sweaters attract cat hair in direct proportion to the darkness of the fabric.

- *Law of Cat Thermodynamics* — Heat flows from a warmer to a cooler body, except in the case of a cat, in which case all heat flows to the cat.

- *Law of Cat Stretching* — A cat will stretch to a distance proportional to the length of the nap just taken.

- *Law of Cat Sleeping* — All cats must sleep with people whenever possible, in a position as uncomfortable for the people involved as is possible for the cat.

- *Law of Cat Elongation* — A cat can make her body long enough to reach just about any countertop that has anything remotely interesting on it.

- *Law of Cat Acceleration* — A cat will accelerate at a constant rate, until he gets good and ready to stop.

- *Law of Dinner Table Attendance* — Cats must attend all meals when anything good is served.

- *Law of Rug Configuration* — No rug may remain in its naturally flat state for very long.

- *Law of Obedience Resistance* — A cat's resistance varies in proportion to a human's desire for her to do something.

- *First Law of Energy Conservation* — Cats know that energy can neither be created nor destroyed and will, therefore, use as little energy as possible.

- *Second Law of Energy Conservation* — Cats also know that energy can only be stored by a lot of napping.

- *Law of Refrigerator Observation* — If a cat watches a refrigerator long enough, someone will come along and take out something good to eat.

- *Law of Electric Blanket Attraction* — Turn on an electric blanket and a cat will jump into bed at the speed of light.

- *Law of Random Comfort Seeking* — A cat will always seek, and usually take over, the most comfortable spot in any given room.

- *Law of Bag / Box Occupancy* — All bags and boxes in a given room must contain a cat within the earliest possible nanosecond.

- *Law of Cat Embarrassment* — A cat's irritation rises in direct proportion to her embarrassment times the amount of human laughter.

- *Law of Milk Consumption* — A cat will drink his weight in milk, squared, just to show you he can.

- *Law of Furniture Replacement* — A cat's desire to scratch furniture is directly proportional to the cost of the furniture.

- *Law of Cat Landing* — A cat will always land in the softest place possible.

- *Law of Fluid Displacement* — A cat immersed in milk will displace her own volume, minus the amount of milk consumed.

- *Law of Cat Disinterest* — A cat's interest level will vary in inverse proportion to the amount of effort a human expends in trying to interest him.

- *Law of Pill Rejection* — Any pill given to a cat has the potential energy to reach escape velocity.

- *Law of Cat Composition* — A cat is composed of Matter + Anti-Matter + It Doesn't Matter.

— Unknown

WHAT CAN WE LEARN FROM CATS?

Cats have figured out how to manage their lives pretty well, especially considering their pecan-sized brains. Or are they walnut-sized? Whatever the nut size, we might be happier if we emulated some cat attitudes and behaviors.

Everything I know I learned from my cat: When you're hungry, eat. When you're tired, nap in a sunbeam. When you go to the vet's, pee on your owner.

— Gary Smith

Cats are intended to teach us that not everything in nature has a purpose.

— Garrison Keillor

A man who carries a cat by the tail learns something he can learn in no other way.

— Mark Twain

Things you can learn from your cat

- The world is your playground.

- Rest and relaxation are keys to happiness. There is always time for a catnap, in a sunbeam whenever possible.

- Always stretch and yawn before you get up.

- Cleanliness is next to godliness. Keep yourself clean and cover your crap.

- "Kneading bread" is good for the soul, and makes you look adorable.

- Always give generously: leaving a dead bird or mouse shows that you care.

- You know you're smarter, so there's no need to prove it all the time.

- A backrub is one of life's great pleasures.

- Don't settle for second-rate food. Be stubborn and maybe you'll get fancy, expensive food.

- Keep your life interesting with variety: one day, ignore people; next day, annoy them.

- Be independent: don't do things just because people want you to.

- Expect to be pampered and treated royally.

- Climb your way to the top.

- Experience life from a different perspective by finding a high perch.

- When in doubt, cop an attitude.

- The family that sleeps together stays together. So curl up really close behind your person's knees or in the crook of their neck and purr, but do not move.

- Remain aloof; don't seem too eager to please.

- Indifference makes you appear less judgmental.

- If you've got something inside that doesn't belong there, like a hairball or bottled-up feelings — get it out.

- See yourself as the lion you are.

- Live life on your own terms.

- If you go out on a limb, try to land on your feet.

There is no human problem which could not be solved if people would simply do as cats advise.

— Gore Vidal (with apologies)

ACKNOWLEDGMENTS

We've made every reasonable effort to locate original sources, obtain permission to use copyright protected content, and supply complete and correct credits. If there are errors or omissions, please contact info@quippery.com so we can address corrections in any subsequent edition.

Twitter
Our heartfelt thanks to all the Twitter users who allowed us to include their great tweets. Please check them all out on Twitter!

Cat silhouettes from www.Vecteezy.com

The mysterious origin of cats
From *The Cat Who Came for Christmas* by Cleveland Amory Trust, copyright © 1987. Reprinted by permission of Little, Brown and Company, an imprint of Hachette Book Group, Inc.

We're sitting here having a chat
Copyright © 2018 by Robert Wilde. All rights reserved. Reprinted by permission of the author.

Common Benefits Of Cat Ownership
Reprinted with permission of The Onion. Copyright © 2018, by Onion, Inc. www.theonion.com

You cannot expect everything even from the friendliest cat. It is still a cat.
From *The Cat Who Came for Christmas* by Cleveland Amory Trust, copyright ©
1987. Reprinted by permission of Little, Brown and Company, an imprint of
Hachette Book Group, Inc.

Cat Seemed Perfectly Content Right Up Until Point He Bolted Out Of Room.
Reprinted with permission of The Onion. Copyright © 2018, by Onion, Inc.
www.theonion.com

*Cat Internally Debates Whether Or Not To Rip Head Off Smaller Creature It
Just Met*
Reprinted with permission of The Onion. Copyright © 2018, by Onion, Inc.
www.theonion.com

House Cat Announces Plans To Just Sit There For 46 Minutes
Reprinted with permission of The Onion. Copyright © 2018, by Onion, Inc.
www.theonion.com

*Cat Looking Out Window, Bird Form Unbelievably Intense Fifth-Of-A-Second
Bond*
Reprinted with permission of The Onion. Copyright © 2018, by Onion, Inc.
www.theonion.com

One of the ways . . .
From *The Cat Who Came for Christmas* by Cleveland Amory Trust, copyright ©
1987. Reprinted by permission of Little, Brown and Company, an imprint of
Hachette Book Group, Inc.

GIVING BACK

We pledge to donate a percentage of our profits in support of planet and people, through the vital work of two nonprofit organizations:

Planet

Since 1951, The Nature Conservancy (www.nature.org) has worked to protect the lands and waters on which all life depends.

People

The David Lynch Foundation (www.davidlynchfoundation.org) supports the health, well-being, and personal development of at-risk students, veterans suffering from PTSD, women and girls who have been the victims of violence, people living with HIV/AIDS, prisoners, and at-risk children in other countries.

DAVID LYNCH
FOUNDATION

MORE FROM QUIPPERY!

If you haven't done so already, please check out:

FUR & GRRR
THE FUNNIEST THINGS PEOPLE HAVE SAID ABOUT
DOGS

And more Quippery books are on the way. Just go to Quippery.com and sign up on our email list. We'll let you know when they're available.

If there's any way we can improve this book, we'd love to hear from you at feedback@quippery.com.

Finally, we'd be grateful for your review on Amazon. Please go to Amazon.com and search for "Quippery."

THANKS FOR READING!

Made in the USA
Las Vegas, NV
10 March 2022

45396531R00125